Lovers of the Place

Monasticism Loose in the Church

Francis Kline, O.C.S.O.

A Liturgical Press Book

THE LITURGICAL PRESS
Collegeville, Minnesota

Cover design by David Manahan, O.S.B. Cover photo from *L'Art Cistercien*, France.

2	3	4	5	6	7	8

Library of Congress Cataloging-in-Publication Data

Kline, Francis, 1948–
    Lovers of the place : monasticism loose in the church / Francis Kline.
        p.   cm.
    Includes bibliographical references.
    ISBN 0–8146–2428–6
    1. Monastic and religious life.   2. Monasticism and religious orders.   I. Title.
BX2435.K55   1997
255—dc20   96–34650
                                                                    CIP

finish by Sunday!
020723

Contents

LOVERS OF THE PLACE

St. Stephen Harding, one of the three founders of Cîteaux,
was a lover of the Rule and of the place.

> *. . . quique amator regulae et loci erat.*
> (*Exordium parvum*, 17:12)

Introduction

This book has enjoyed a long birthing. I say enjoyed, because surprise and delight have greeted it at every turn all along the way to completion. Irish Trappists asked me to participate in a workshop on formation in 1990. I agreed, since the topic assigned to me was fascinating: *new images of the monastic life.* I foresaw immediately that I could not come up with completely new ideas, but I might be able to reinvent some old thinking and adapt it to some of the problem areas which newcomers to monastic life in our time have identified. The result was a manuscript of three longish essays based on three major dialectics: the desert and the garden, stability and mobility, and renunciation passing to marginality. The workshop material was well received and published privately by the Irish for their benefit, together with the material of the other presenters. It achieved a modest success in our Order, the Trappists, or, the Cistercians of the Strict Observance.

But that was not to be the end. Michael Downey, who has acted as catalyst for so many invigorating publications in spirituality in recent years, suggested to me that "the manuscript" might have a future, since monastic spirituality was supporting an abiding interest in these post-Merton days. Michael and I had several conversations on the topic of cracking open the monastic treasury so that others in the Church might blessedly loot its contents. Should there even be a monasticism today, we asked, with cloisters and silence and withdrawal? In the throes of wild speculation it seemed a legitimate question, although a disturbing one to someone of my classically oriented and conservative mind. I was haunted by the fact that the new self-understanding of the Church given at Vatican II had not yet taken good root. It was still being crowded out by a dense overgrowth of old perceptions however noble they may have been. And Pope Paul VI remained an enigmatic though beloved figure, making retreats at monasteries and writing letters to meetings and general chapters of monastics, urging them to open their charism to the wider Church. The central question was, how to share something that didn't seem to want to be shared but only joined. After all, you can't live monastic life outside a monastery complex, or can you?

I had always steered away from anything but the most orthodox monasticism. Popularizations and easy access to ancient wisdom have never appealed to me. So I stalled at Michael Downey's suggestion of rewriting my manuscript. My thoughts and statements made in our conversations had not yet passed into my life. They were not yet digested. But the years of experience, now that I had become an abbot of a monastery, were effecting in me what the mind could not do unaided.

In the monastery where I now live, many people who come to make retreats ask: "How can I share more deeply in your life without actually living here? Are a couple of retreats a year enough?" I have developed answers to these questions in numerous interviews with people whose grace I cannot deny. The Holy Spirit speaks through them and I can no longer avoid certain affirmative answers about the sharing of the monastic charism, certainly by the baptized, and even by the married.

Then there is my beloved community of Mepkin, whose distinctive style of hospitality has shown me how involved retreatants can become with a community without affecting adversely its grace and prayer. Mepkin, not without purpose in the Spirit's plans, I'm sure, is located in the Diocese of Charleston, whose bishop, David B. Thompson, convoked a most extraordinary synod in 1990. It concluded in 1995, but only after including me and some of the community in the most challenging debates I have ever known. For it was a question not of preaching monasticism, but of struggling with difficult contemporary Church problems and searching the monastic tradition for answers, as well as the wider and more recent tradition. As I came to appreciate the superabundant grace bestowed on the baptized during the synod, I saw the vision which must have inspired the writers of *Lumen gentium* and *Gaudium et spes*—a cloud of witnesses summoned from every walk of life in a universal call to holiness. In the crucible of hard work done reluctantly apart from monastery concerns for the sake of the Church, I feel that the Spirit has offered to me something new for my own monastic life, which has always been refreshing and new for me.

A new book, incorporating large portions of the original manuscript, now became a possibility after a hiatus of almost three years. I began to work, but with many false starts. For I needed a governing image, a unifying idea, a voice of poetic imagination to draw together my disparate thoughts on this difficult topic. I found it in the vision of the Church as communion in a vast building of great architecture. Instead of a reasoned treatise acceptable to the academy, I decided on a style of articulation far more narrative and more dependent on poetic principles, where images could be heaped up and organized around an experience of conversion.

My first chapter, therefore, is an allegory of the Church, as broad and inclusive as I could get it, yet with certain and firm demands of gospel living as its entrance requirements. The monastic community takes its place on an equal basis with the other groups in the assembly. It is neither the holiest group, nor the underprivileged minority. Its place can only be understood by a knowledge of the process of living the gospel and being transformed by it in faith, hope and love.

In chapter two, I break open the allegory and suggest particular interpretations to the general happenings in the hall of the building. Here, monasticism is located not at the top of the Church, but as a leaven in its midst with especial regard to the new ecclesiology prompted by the conciliar documents.

As I continue the interpretation of the allegory in chapter three, I make a list of the essential characteristics of monastic living based on the tradition, but with an eye to a contemporary hermeneutic, as well as the possibility of living the monastic charism beyond the cloister.

In chapters four, five and six, I further explore the monastic tradition by offering the three basic images that formed the original manuscript. But this imagery, unlike the first attempt, is now built around a commentary on the central doctrine of the Rule of St. Benedict, the seventh chapter on the twelve steps of humility. In this part of the book, I view monastic doctrine in the context of a lifetime, and what transformations in Christ are wrought there by the living of the Rule. After all, we can fully expect to realize goals and effect behavioral changes in a tradition of such richness. Thus, chapter four weaves the imagery of the Desert and the Garden around the first three steps of humility. Chapter five adopts the opposing energies of stability and mobility to discuss the idea of the Promised Land in the light of steps four through eight. And in chapter six, a commentary on the final steps of humility on silence, I am able to draw together the many loose ends of the discussion by seeing how marginality is really the built-in goal of the monastic. For monastics become marginal not only to the society from which they come, and this includes the Church under the guidance of the bishops which nourished them before monastic life, but, paradoxically, to monastic structures themselves. For monastic ascesis, in its silence and quiet suffering, pushes a monastic to the very edge of the monastery itself. The monastics, if they are faithful to Christ, come to affirm the very ecclesiology which seems to threaten them. They do this by living to the full Christ's own marginalization in his paschal mystery. He left the world, only to take it all to himself. In this way, the monastics are seen to straddle the monastery and the Church in a tension that defies definitions and rules. The final chapter returns to the initial allegory and offers some considerations about the perennial monastic charism and how it relates to a new understanding of the Church.

The whole purpose of the book is to make available to the Church the riches of the monastic tradition. And as I explore this theme, I come to discover that monasticism can renew itself in its very essence by giving of itself for the sake of the Church. In looking to the baptized, who discern in the monastic way their own journey, we return to the Church itself which gave us birth and from where we can take new energies for the lonely journey ahead. Having had their own treasury looted by the baptized, the monastics find themselves loose in a world which has become more and more their place and their home. How we belong to the Church, and what we can give to the Church in a more obvious way—these two aims find ample development in these pages.

Although written from a Roman Catholic perspective, the insertion of monastic spirituality into a wider Church will surely suggest further avenues of development for other Christian believers, as well as those without creedal affiliation. A full treatment of the ecumenicity of the monastic tradition is a book yet to be written.

Michael Downey deserves the lion's share of my gratitude for believing in me and in this book when I thought I had no time for such a venture. My monastic communities of Gethsemani, where I was raised as a monk, and Mepkin which is now my home, show a face on every page. Cornelius Justice and Nivard Kinsella, of the monasteries of Mt. Melleray and Roscrea in Ireland initiated the project some six years ago. Ladislas Örsy, S.J., Martin Iott, O.P., and the Reverend Fred Heckel, now my brother in community, shared with me the excitement of the first drafts; and Robert Durback offered helpful comments on the manuscript as it neared completion. The Reverend Patrick Caverly of Altamonte Springs, Florida, has been a source of constant encouragement; the Reverend Frank Muscolino of Birmingham, Alabama, shared with me his home for the crucial writing of chapters two and three. πThe Reverend Ralph Quane helped with proofreading and compiled the index. My own brothers at Mepkin, Father Aelred Hagan and Brother Stanislaus Gumula, as well as faithful Brother Joshua Shlosberg and the entire Mepkin community, supported my work on the book as well as my various activities in and out of the monastery. Their convictions about the Church of today and how monasticism fits into it, I trust, find some voice here.

Their own monastic witness has been, and continues to be for me, a fertile matrix for further development. Bishop Thompson, Monsignor Sam Miglarese and Sister Bridget Sullivan and the entire staff of the Synod of Charleston have been a constant source of encouragement and challenge to my understanding of Church. To all of these, my prayers, thanks and honor.

Francis Kline, O.C.S.O.
Mepkin Abbey
Moncks Corner, South Carolina
Pentecost 1995

CHAPTER ONE

At the Gates: An Allegory

It towers above the *polis* like Notre Dame in Paris, but it is not a church building with a spire, cross or bells. Its architecture is monumental, evidently holding thousands of people, but it is not like a stadium open to the elements, or a convention center with a nondescript bulk. By its very color on the skyline of the city, you know it is different—feminine patina greens and browns with greys and pinks bespeaking an altogether special stone, not quarried locally, and adorned with copper. It is a building that immediately poses questions even as it decorates the urban center.

But what is it? Government buildings would not parade so lavish or foreign a facade which the common people could not relate to. Perhaps it is something like the fourth-century buildings of Constantine with their columns, colonnades and their overripe mosaics and carvings dear to the Roman populace. Or perhaps it is something closer to our own time: late Victorian style from the closing years of the last century, wearing a comfortable opulence, even a flamboyance, but still restrained by meanings and assurances of its culture's religious beliefs and place in the world. Might it be London's Royal Albert Hall or the old Trocaderó of Paris? Yet, our building is too solemn to be an entertainment place. It has the foreboding of a museum, but no banners rustle outside in the breeze to indicate a major exhibition going on or even to identify itself to the passersby. Besides, there are no vendors at its entrances, or tour buses anywhere to be seen. There is something of the off-limits appearance of a hospital, but it lacks the hospital's sterile and stern practicality. The architecture is too playful, too fantastic, not at all pedestrian.

Like the Royal Albert Hall, it may be a concert auditorium, but if so, there is more than just music that happens there. Perhaps it is a temple dedicated to all the arts or the very dignity and universality of the human person—a sort of cosmic UNESCO building. But whatever its meaning and purpose, it is both out of place in its surroundings, because there is nothing else like it, and, at the same time, it bespeaks a presence both massive and calm, peaceful and self-contained. It is not threatened or made to feel uncomfortable by its strangeness. It even seems impervious to the noncomprehension of the crowd.

As one gets closer to the edifice by descending into its home in the burrow-like streets deep in the heart of the old city, its adornments come into high relief. Arcane inscriptions, faces, masks, statues and sculpted objects, such as flowers, fruits and vines cover the exterior. Many are recognizable as bread, grapes, olives and the like. Obviously, these are symbols of what goes on inside. These are comfortable symbols, signs of elemental life and love. But there are also scenes depicting human compassion in the service of the blind and the lame, the poor and the prisoner. More mysterious and less reassuring are the scenes of agony and suffering: figures weeping and wailing at the violence done to them by others or perhaps themselves. Some look like medieval judgment scenes, others like gargoyles, half human, half monstrous. Figures of unfathomable majesty and wisdom stand opposite the jeering and the silly—a veritable palimpsest of the human story. Here there is greed as well as nobility, dignity as well as corruption.

Outside the building stand large crowds milling about the entrances. Many seem to be going in; just as many are exiting. Upon closer inspection, clusters of people can be seen looking up and admiring the facade. They are speaking together about the building and what goes on inside it. Some boast about their past visits and what they experienced. "I used to belong as a child, but as I grew older, all that dogma turned me off.

Now I think I want to enter again." Says another, "I'm tired of the hauteur, the way they pretend to have all the answers, the total and only true response to life, barring none. It's not for me." A third says that she has admired it all her life from afar. But where she grew up, there was no thought of joining. But now, after years of watching its unity, its diversity, its authenticity, even its foibles, she feels as though this were home. It is time for her to go in. Yet another asks what happens inside, and, much to his and everyone's surprise, no one can exactly say. "There are events, services, gatherings," says one, "but that's not it. It's a way of life, a way to love, a system of beliefs which becomes one belief."

The Voice

Pushing forward past the groups of people standing at some distance from the entrance, I notice immediate reactions in myself. From the building I hear sounds that awaken my ears. I'm not sure if it's music or speaking. Like Christmas carols hanging in the air around a department store's entrance, these sounds seem not to affect the crowd, that is, no one seems to be standing around listening. But whatever it is, the sound is affecting me. I want to get closer so as to identify it. Even while I ponder it, it thrills me. I stand still and strain to listen, even while I am jostled by the crowd. I can make out a grand chorus with organ or orchestra. Is this a performance of Elgar's *The Dream of Gerontius* when the soul first hears the chorus of the Angelicals? But even while I can begin to identify music, there is some other source of sound beyond my ability to describe. It is a Voice, but it is uttering no word I can understand. Yet I hear it and my heart responds.

And now I must speak of an experience as clear as it is strange. Before I realized that the Voice was beckoning me, I became aware of a precipice of emotion over whose edge I was peering. Great was that fall from a mountain stronghold which I had spent years building and defending! I had shut myself up inside my own impregnable tower and only part of me, the outward part, all painted and appointed, would venture forth to see and to hear and to live as a social being. But the real I, the seat of love and commitment, remained safely locked away. Now I realized to my horror, that my maiden self was at the castle door, about to cross the moat, approach the edge and fly away, summoned by the Voice.

To do what and to go where, I had no idea, nor did I care. For the impossible had occurred. The high mountain pass had been breached. Some Judith had charmed her way in, her treachery unsuspected. And now I had the unmistakable feeling of being violated, beheaded even, of being won over in a way no love had ever managed to do before. It was the knowledge of having been entered and encountered that mattered more than anything else. And I could not help myself or reassert my sovereignty. For some unobvious but long-intuited time mechanism had sounded and I was summoned forth. Despite the ravage of it, I felt clean, if frightened; relieved, if naked, and the exhilaration of freedom was matched only by the energy it released.

But my defense roused itself. The whips of internal discipline were cracked, first over my head, and then cruelly applied to my heart. Standing there in the crowd, my struggle in bleeding pain went unnoticed. My bloodied shirt oozed like a spring. For a moment, I recognized my surroundings: Broad St., narrow Baxter St. at the corner, smog-filled sky, mid-morning, people with the look of passersby on their faces. "Wake up, man," I told myself. *Like a dream one wakes from, O Lord*—I heard the Chorus singing in words I could suddenly understand. "Hold onto reality," I shouted. *One day within your courts* came the Chorus. "You have a life here, you are not some robot." *Like the deer, yearning for running streams . . . .*

At the same moment, reeling from the horror of this decisional rack pulling at my being, I seemed to see in the sky above a diagram of my situation. It was neat and clear, with clean lines and primary colors. I saw that this drawing was mine. It did not relate to the folks around me, only to me, the Voice and the Building. I knew that this was my crossroads, the Hall of Decision, the way to everlasting love, if I chose it, or the descent into diminishment, if I rejected it. I saw this but I could not choose, I could only comprehend. And with the comprehension came the sights and smells, all around the diagram, of a meadow on a June day. I could even hear the bees in the clover. So there was no foreign or artificial noise or other influence from the city that could affect me. This decision would have to be a thing of stillness, beauty, made in utter peace, not part of the chaos around and below me.

Then a new apparition. I noticed a young man, thin lipped, of slight build, stylish as to dress and appearance, looking at me with interest. Did he realize what was happening to me? Was he offering help? No, he just stood there looking at me. In the awkwardness of the moment, I was drawn to his eyes. He had chestnut brown eyes that were familiar, like eyes I have loved. But they were troubling, because, while they were looking at me inappropriately for a stranger (but was he a stranger?) they were without intention. Here was a person who had lost his way . . . had bought a cheap bill of goods and was paying the hefty price for paltry trinkets with his own life blood. His face and his lips were pale from the draining. He could not take my stare, but kept looking back. I pitied him, even as I loved him, and as the two emotions came together, the thunder struck and it began to rain knowledge. Christ Almighty! the eyes were my own. The empty man was myself, and the eyes were the eyes of a sinner.

Screaming with dread and revulsion, I bolted out of my paralysis and ran toward the Building. With a rush of air coming from the Building, music met me and the Voice became audible and understandable. It was singing of love, in what language, I did not know. But the message was *Come in here and live.*

The Atrium

The enormous height of the atrium hushed all the noise of the bustle and traffic of the street. Here, the crowds on the floor made no more than a low drone, as if they were the smallest bees on flowers hidden in the grass. The space and the grandeur of the upward vaults clothed themselves with silence and dignity. Only an occasional outburst or explosion of sound made one aware of any particularity on the floor below.

There was motion, too, in the majesty, since the hall curved, revealing the jutting angles of the cornices and columns as it did so. You could only suspect the immensity of the building around the part of the curve you could not see. Within, in each pair of columns, was a monumental door, such as you see in Greek revival public buildings of the European and American eighteenth and nineteenth centuries. How many of these continued around the curve, I could not guess. Sunlight streaming down through square clerestory windows cast long rays of metallic sunshine across the hall, like rods of gleaming steel supporting the building. Meanwhile, the doors attracted my attention, for they were obviously entrances into some other hall or inner auditorium. Around each doorway, the crowd had left a space, as if out of respect for it, or for those people who formed a small but steady stream in and out of them. I looked at these for a while, but my gaze was soon drawn away from the solemn doors and their mystery and toward the bustling activity of the atrium where the majority of the people were engaged in sundry activities. Soon caught up into this other life, the doors faded into second place.

The crowd seemed intent on this world of the foyer. The peace of the upper spaces was swallowed up by the localized acoustical environment. Thick in the crowd were low shops, stalls and vendors of every description. Bright lights and crystal chandeliers burned in low-ceilinged cells which housed display cases of jewelry, rings, and ornaments for both men and women. Clothes, formal wear and sports wear shops were also in abundance. Folks could be seen trying things on, shining in their own exuberant health and well-being. These were people of importance, but what they were important to, in what was only the atrium of this great building, was unclear to me. Young people clustered around stalls blaring their music. Like children following the Pied Piper, they stood mesmerized in their uniformly garish outfits. At the food stalls, they came alive, laughing and hollering, as the boys chased the girls.

Elsewhere, individuals could be seen alone with some object they had just purchased. They stood admiring them idol-like. To have something valuable and precious was clearly of great significance to these folks. They seemed to have no inter-est in the crowds of people around them. Others were gathered in small clusters around similarly acquired items. Chatting and pointing out details of their possessions, they were altogether as far removed from the atrium and its purpose as the single idol worshippers.

Loud cheers and clapping punctuated the din in the air on the floor of the atrium. Stalls with games and contests in progress attracted small crowds of very devoted fans and par-ticipants alike. It looked as though in each game, the crowd di-vided themselves into two sides, deciding now for this contestant, now that one. The ferocity of the devotion to their chosen cause far outweighed the purpose of the game, incon-gruous as it was in such a place. But the games gave their lives meaning, and the meaning released energy that propelled them forward in their unthinking activity. More somber and calculat-ing persons could be seen at stalls where betting for distant events was received. Here, horse races were not the sport, but the outcome of ideological debates, appointments to posts, de-cisions concerning rules and regulations, etc. The folks grouped around these stalls were intensely absorbed, having subordi-nates and staffers to maneuver their positions with some great office that was located elsewhere, not in the building.

The most serious business was carried on further away from the doors. And here the colors of the garb grew propor-tionately brighter and more ceremonial. Piping, lace, satins and silks swished on men and women alike. Positions delin-eated by clothing were impossible to distinguish. Importance, however, seemed to be attached to the distinction of the outfit. The finer the cut, the more precious the material, the more stately the bearing, the mien more imposing. Some of the more elegantly dressed persons had small numbers of attendants scurrying off to the vendors and returning with small bundles of trinkets or edibles. Others involved themselves in a more deadly game, standing at bureaus, manipulating graphs and maps showing worldwide distribution of food and clothing needed by millions of people. Significantly, these places were faced away from the solemn doors and looking outward to the street.

Everywhere, the contrasts were great—small people munching goodies, great people walking in stately decorum, busy people hurrying to and fro, lazy people enjoying a seat at one of the many cafés, watching the world go by. Few ventured near the solemn doors, where a cautious distance was always observed.

Watching the thin but steady stream of persons entering the doors, I noticed that none of them possessed anything, or held anything as they entered—no snacks, no packages, no bundles, and certainly no casual companions from the crowd. And you had to take off whatever garb you were wearing and strip down to a grey undergarment which everyone seemed to have on beneath their clothes. Entering the doors was obviously a serious business. Occasionally, there would be a small crowd accompanying someone close to the door. Couples could also be seen, a man and a woman joining hands with the intention of entering. Then, the support group would halt before the entrance, always observing some distance, as if one might get contaminated with the air of the world inside and not be acceptable in the carnival atmosphere of the atrium. And then, in an incredible silence which the low din of the atrium could not destroy, the person(s) would enter the hall all alone, not to be seen in the same way again.

Of those exiting, for indeed, people were coming out of the doors, little need be said. When they came out in groups of two or three, they made loud noise, murmurings and criticisms, angry and biting. They also seemed to be reclothed in the loudest of colors, proclaiming to all that they belonged to the atrium and had adopted its uniform. It was not long before they mingled with the vendors, the game players and all the other fun seekers in the atrium. They quickly met up with friends whom they had left on their entrance. How long they had been on the other side of the doors was anybody's guess. But when they came out, what they had seen or heard had not pleased them. They seemed determined to reestablish themselves in the thick and heavy atmosphere of the floor of the atrium.

Nevertheless, some other folks would emerge from the doors, but with no crowd to meet them. They would slip anonymously by, unobtrusively, singly, or in couples, in the plainest of costume and mingle themselves with the crowd. These, I'm told, would even make their way, practically unnoticed, out onto the street. Their exit from the building went unobserved due to their lack of complaining, their lack of discussion about the building and its meaning. They simply slipped away with unsuspected purpose into the larger world.

As I made my way around the lofty curve of the atrium, I observed that certain doors were only for single persons, and others were only for married (marriageable?) couples. Gradually, I became aware that one could choose the door that suited one best, further complicating the question of what went on inside or what one would see inside. Did compartments, matching the selectivity of the doors, keep groups of people separated even within the hall? Or were they all mingled, and if so, what purpose did the distinguishing doors serve? Did something occur in the person that forever marked them out, even in the vast assembly hall? Or was it vast at all? This building held such mystery, that perhaps it was paradoxically diminutive after the enormity of the atrium. Or could it be vastly larger than the atrium, defying all perspective like outer space?

There was only one way to find out. And my growing curiosity about the hall coincided with an ever increasing urge from the Voice to enter. I set about to reflect on the matter. The great puzzle was obviously the atrium itself. Though it was clearly an entrance into mystery and meaning from the foggy world outside, it nevertheless set up for itself a major obstacle in its own senseless activity. Its loftiness and beauty were catalysts enough to go further in to the doors. Yet, why was the majority satisfied with the pleasurable pastimes and the innocent diversions so far from the solemn doors with which they occupied themselves? True enough, some folks were entering the doors, and their reverence was palpable. What of the crowd? Why could they not be reverent, or less flippant, or less absorbed? Pondering these insolubles with head lowered and feet scuffing the floor, I noticed the smeared brown stain that seemed to be everywhere on the white marble. So uniform was it, as if manna had fallen and longed to be picked up, that I wondered what substance had been spilled from the vendors' stalls and walked on so nonchalantly as to make such an even stain. I looked up in my quandary, and there, in the full sunlight streaming in from the clerestory windows, I beheld the cross and blood dripping from it, like a shower, onto the unthinking crowd. The people continued their shopping, their betting, their eating, with never a beat skipped in their pursuits. They did not notice the shower. Could they not see the cross? I looked again at the floor. It was becoming wet and the smears were glistening. I looked around me again. No comprehension. Only the shuffling of feet, which grew louder in my ears, and the louder it became, the more horrific did the situation grow in my mind. And with the cacophonous shuffling of feet, came the knowledge that the stalls, and the vendors and all the games had grown up in the atrium precisely to blunt the attention as to what was really happening. And with that awful inattention, the cross could not be seen. And the shower could be so abused. And the love of God could be so trampled underfoot. One did not stand on this floor with innocence or insouciance. And of a sudden, it came to me that the serious game players were walking on it with deliberate intent. The atrium was supposed to be an introduction and welcoming place into God's great hall. It had become the place where God continued to suffer the mindlessness of his people. I needed confirmation. I looked at those who were entering the doors. They were clutching handkerchiefs and dabbing their faces carefully. I hadn't fathomed what this action might mean, or if they had been crying. Now I knew. The atrium was not a neutral place with mindless, harmless *divertissements* for a bored populace. It was already a place of judgment. With sober care, taking out my handkerchief, but with a sense of great urgency, I approached the doors. I thought of his passion and death. And I believed in his resurrection. I entered the doors, in the name of the Father, the Son, and the Holy Spirit.

Inside the Hall

I was thrust into the center of it. Around me crowded faces, and around my ears passed singing voices and majestic chords from instruments and percussion. Though there were no lamps, the brightness of the light blinded me for a while, and I could not avoid it, not even by shielding my eyes. The ground under me constantly resonated with the sound, as if from some organ bourdon, not an unpleasant sensation. The swish of robes, all in white, as if in constant movement could be heard even in the midst of the music. With all my senses whirling, I stumbled, but did not fall. Sweet, angelic hands which yet were warm and tactile steadied me and soothed my face, when I realized that my whole body had been twisting faster than I could imagine. The hands were bringing the motion to a halt.

What I saw when I came to rest were choirs of beings, all their eyes on me. I bolted, trying to get out of the center, but every place was the center. When, in my confusion, I tried to find a place where I could hide, I realized that I should stay where I was. They were all singing, and I was singing. I was in the midst of the singing chorus, but I could yet hear the grand acoustics of the hall, as if I were deep down the nave from the sanctuary of a great cathedral. Here, every place was the sanctuary, yet the majesty of distance and the ability to take in the whole scene at once remained.

As my eyes adjusted to the immensity of the place, I began to see how the groups of beings were arranged around the center. Their garments seemed to distinguish them one group from the other. From pale, almost transparent robes to brilliant greens, yellows and scarlets, the color scheme wound its way around the hall. The colors of the garments were enhanced by the richness of the windows circling the hall high above. From clear glass to ever deepening hues, the windows, conveying shafts of light to the floor below, matched the gradations of the colors. The greens were reinforced by light from green windows above; the reds were the same, and so on. A many colored light, streaming from the high windows fell first of all on the Glory in the center, or was the Glory illuminating the windows from within the hall? The light seemed to arc from the Glory to the windows, and from the arc, the beings took their radiance. As I looked more intently at the groupings, I saw that the brightly colored robes belonged to the baptized, the married, the families. Their employments were mirrored in the various shades of their garments: teachers, business people, crafts people, laborers and all manner of workers, health care providers, nurses and doctors. All around the circle ministered the bishops, the priests, the deacons and ministers. They mingled in and among the groupings singly and in pairs, distinguishable only by their head gear. The bishops were the most obvious. Some of these were seen to be serving near the floor, as if washing the feet of the beings. Their miters shone. The religious could be seen, too, serving all the others. The more they moved among the beings in their service, the brighter their colors, as if they were to be grouped with baptized and the married. Curiously, the more monastic and separated beings wore garments of lighter and paler shades. Above them, their windows were clear glass. An inner light seemed to emanate very weakly from beneath their garments, but as a whole, they were in shadow as if in winter light. The light from the Glory at the center or from the windows above was not aimed at them for the moment. I wondered what would happen if the light should ever shift in their direction. Could any eyes behold it?

So, as I surveyed the whole scene, loving it all the while, and feeling continually more comfortable with a stirring sense of well-being, like nothing I had ever before experienced, I knew that my blessing was in the beings that I beheld, and that theirs, somehow, was in mine. But I cannot describe how the multiplicity which I saw became one, and how, though each person had their place according to their garments, the mingling of the different groupings created a constantly shifting rainbow of colors among the choirs, and still, they were not disordered. The assembly assumed the appearance of the shining coat of a great animal whose frame and muscles rippled beneath the undulating skin. For this community was alive and on the move as one, although we were not conscious of spatial flight. This was not a herd in stampede, but a galaxy in motion.

Though I had thought, at first, that all eyes were on me, I could now see that every eye was on the Lamb. And even as the music pulsated in every breast and moved mouths and bodies with rhythmic swinging, a stillness overcame it around the Lamb. The way we could see the Lamb, for his brightness was such that you could not look directly on him immediately, was to look at the figures surrounding him. They both filtered and prepared the brightness for our eyes. These were the Virgin Mary and John the Baptist. They, too, were filled with the brightness, so that light seemed to emanate from them personally, but it was not so. Neither were they still, but danced in ritual fashion around the circle, catching and throwing light and insight from the Lamb. The Word of God, living and active in them and between them, was the light. The weight of knowledge of God's mystery was thus no heavy thing, but a game of living light, with its own rhythm and steps. After watching this action, we saw the Word as light being thrown to various persons in the choirs, till our eyes became used to sparkling rays of constantly moving crystal. The Virgin and St. John showed the others how to play the game, and they assumed such a preeminence because they knew the Lamb best, and had the longest, deepest and most intimate time (kairos) with him. The light play illumined the Four Living Creatures passing the rays all around them in a gradually growing circle. The whole assembly was inundated with the successive waves of light, showing, as it flowed, the various hues and shapes of the beings—not that they had been in darkness, but that the light revealed all their dimensions, more than three, to our ever-growing eyes. Still, the monastics drew less light to themselves. Among them, the light stilled itself and its waves washed over them in a dead calm.

And now, despite the stillness, there was Glory, the motion of waves and high seas, the crash of cymbals like the surf against the rocks. The Lamb was opening a book, and as he opened and turned the pages, ages and epochs of history fell out, and all the eyes could read them, and the music grew louder and fuller. Yet, our ears could receive it as if finding room for more food.

After a time, the stare of the Lamb released my eyes to the Glory. I had not seen it for the Lamb, but now the Lamb led my eyes to it. The thrill of mountains, the ecstasy of love, the warmth of joy, the pride of the parent all claimed the space of my poor heart. As I looked at the glow, which I mistakenly thought had spatial boundaries, I was transported into an endless glassy sea with low clouds of gold on the horizon. Azure and gold, and all the sensations of warmth and ceaseless tropical life filled my brain. This was a place of rest, and, mysteriously, the source of all growth. The presence of the Almighty was . . . but this phrase tries to describe what cannot be described. Rather, we were all in the presence of the Almighty. Of time, I can say nothing, for there was no time, or rather it was suspended, and the very fact that I can describe the sensation of no heartbeat, no moment passing on to the next, indicates the miraculous nature of this experience. Of space, I know that I was aware of the choirs and the heavenly court, but that nothing could take up any space of the Almighty.

For half an hour, all was still, and yet all ate and drank of this presence. For an instant, the monastics grew luminous as the assembly continued to absorb the light. For a brief moment, a piercing arrow of light and flame arced across the hall connecting them with the Lamb and their windows above. With a shout, the assembly covered their eyes, as a ray of the purest flame, as if from some shooting star, had passed through the hall. The monastics rose to meet it in one bullet-like point. Then it passed. They fell down as if struck. And the hall seemed to grow dark after its passage only to reveal the undulating lesser light, rich in earthier color, continuing in waves around the hall. There was silence. But the monastics began a low hum in the ghostliest of voices that grew in content as the other groups began to sing with them. A new movement was about to break upon us as the music continued to swell.

Then the Glory erupted from its place in a shower of cascading light, as if the sea were being poured from a crystal vault above. The sound of it was like the crash of cymbals, or like the surf against rocks. The choruses of beings rose at once with a shout, though in harmony. (The harmony was something I thought I recognized, or, at least, could be given to notation, but later, as I attempted it, I could not write it down.) Over waves of words in countless tongues, there arose the unmistakable refrain: "Worthy is the Lamb that was slaughtered to receive power and wealth and wisdom and might and honor and glory and blessing" (Rev 5:12b).[1] And as the Lamb bowed to the Glory, all in unison sang:

> "To the one seated on the throne and to the Lamb be blessing and honor and glory and might forever and ever" (Rev 5:13b)!

How long the praise endured can never be measured. But time entered the hall again, and, like a performance, the praise ended. It faded from view. It did not disappear, as if it were a mirage. It was we who left it. And although we remained in the hall, we, the choirs of mortals, the Glory was no longer there. Something in us no longer had the capacity to bear it. With a cold shock of recognition, I knew that what we had experienced was a sacrament—an enhanced and momentary encounter with God in Christ, by means of a sign. And here the sign was praise. It was the Eucharist, the offering of Christ, and all that is his Body, to the Glory, to the Father. And we would go forever after, the richer and the poorer for it.

There was some low talking. Many were seen to be falling to prayer on their knees, or in a sitting position on the floor, or walking off to a quiet corner of the hall. Gradually, some began to make their way to the exits. It was then that we realized that those who remained were the saints. We had been celebrating the liturgy with the whole host of heaven.

They had joined us, or rather, we had joined them, and they mingled with us with neither rank, nor favor of light, but only with their virtues girded about them like loincloths beneath their outer garments of color. We now realized that their virtues had been the light of God, hidden from our eyes. They had grouped themselves with us according to their office in the Church. In our contemplation of this marvel, we noticed humble looking figures descending to the floor in prayer around the Glory. One small woman had a special light around her, but her face could not be seen. The Lamb shone more brightly towards her, and, in her direction, the Glory made a pathway.

[1] This and all subsequent Scripture citations are taken from the *NRSV* Bible unless otherwise indicated.

Occasionally and most disturbingly, clusters of folks engaged in loud talking could be seen angrily making their way out, apparently not realizing what had happened to them. Obviously, these were headed for the lesser life in the atrium. And sometimes shrill laughter, either from gossip, ribaldry or scorn, rose up from small groups, and these, too, made their way to the exits. Not at home with the air of heaven, they naturally gravitated to the thicker atmosphere of the flesh. No condemnation, or looks of disapproval followed them, only the most profound pity and sadness. The noise of them indicated their whereabouts. You did not even have to look unless you wanted to avoid their rude passage, which often resulted in kicks and shoves aimed at those at prayer. But, on the part of the committed no fear obtained, because it was clear that this hall could not contain unwilling spirits. No unknowing person could remain for long. No one who doubted the love of God could abide the presence of the Glory, which continued to glow in its place. Like the sword at the entrance to the garden, the presence of God made tolerance impossible for any but those who loved it.

We lingered as long as we could. No verbal contact united us, yet we felt an inner communion. At some signal, whether from without or within, I know not which, we slowly rose as one. We knew, from the gentle tugging we felt, that our time here was at an end. We must make our way to the doors and so back to the world. Far from being sad, we were content to do this, even glad to do it. For great joy had seized us, knowing that Christ would go before us and we would have meetings like this again. We sensed, too, that we would be returning to the building at his bidding. But now, we were to do his work—that work which had distinguished our groupings in the hall. Turning neither to the right nor to the left, whether in the atrium or on the streets of the world, we were to keep our gaze fixed on him who loves us. Deep into the heart of the world we were to go, where the struggle for the hearts of mortals goes on day and night, where God's salvation is worked out in every human experience, where the passion of Christ continues, and where his resurrection is experienced.

+ Where the passion or Christ continues and where his resurrection is experienced.

By the time we made our way to the doors, we were actually hurrying. Silently and unobtrusively, we traversed the atrium. There, a sad scene awaited us. The doubters and the scoffers had taken up again their lives among the vendors and the booths. Their crass loudness was all the more offensive to our ears unaccustomed now to anything but the heavenly liturgy. No one voiced the question, yet I'm sure it was on all our minds. Would time, and the repeated urge to enter the hall eventually save them, or condemn them? Would repeated forays into the hall lead them to the Glory, and if so, could they continue with impunity to reject the love of God? Would one time be their last, when, afterward, they would enter forever the exterior darkness?

The questioning quickly ended as the atrium gave way to the outside, and the challenge of Christ's beloved world awaited us. To our various tasks we went, silent like the moonlight on a winter field. Trusting in him and holding fast to one another, we took our stations in our own places until the summons.

CHAPTER TWO

Opening the Gates:
The Allegory Explained

interesting.

The allegory presented in the first chapter is a convenient way to look at the Church in the light of a new ecclesiology brought about by the Vatican Council. Interpreting that allegory may help us to arrive at some fresh reflections on the relationship between the monastic tradition and the wider Church. But it can also stimulate new speculation, as monastics and the baptized interact on each other, on the Church as the journey from personal conversion to an ever increasing incorporation into the body of Christ for the sake of the world.

As we follow the path of the young man from outside the building into the atrium and further into the hall, several themes will show themselves. We notice the transformation from personal preoccupation to wonderment at the larger world of the Church paradoxically inside the building. The theme of wider horizons appearing only through the structures of discipline and constraints will be a constant throughout the allegory. The mere surface interpretation of reality leads also to the interiorization of values, by which all other situations are understood. The Church as communion, a commonplace in theology in recent times, becomes dramatized in the wasteful occupations of the atrium, so that what appears to be important in church life can often distract from the true work of becoming part of Christ's paschal mystery. Likewise, the move from the periphery to the center where the Glory is, will reinforce the paradox of the Church. The glory, as it extends to more and more people through the instrumentation of individuals, appears to be fixed in one place—"the place where your glory abides" (Ps 26:8). Actually, it is an ever-expanding reality, moving inexorably throughout the world by the apostolic peregrinations of its members. Even the concept of "place" becomes fluid. The love of the place, that is, the love of one's place in the Church, one's spirituality, even though we must leave it on one level, never lessens but becomes increasingly inclusive, drawing the baptized into a wider and larger personhood and making them into vessels of glory, which is the direct work of God. Finally, the structure of the monastic life acts as a support for this divinization, and, as such, can be shared by monastics with the larger Church. This more comprehensive participation in the gifts of God and in the very life of God must be seen as the work of the Vatican Council as it prepares to lead the Church into a more effective dialogue with the world and thus to a new evangelization. Let us proceed then with the explanation of the allegory.

The Outside and the Atrium

The Church does not unfold its mystery all at once to the aspirant. The process begins with the investigation of an institution which attracts and repels many people. But as inner prejudices fall away, and as compelling attraction emerges in the heart and mind, the Church gradually becomes approachable to even the most questioning person. We can be talking here of cradle Catholics or any person of whatever denomination, who comes to a deeper understanding of what the Christian Church really is. Cultural yearnings, where the instinct goes further than the mind, are often a part of a person's search for deeper meaning. Liturgy constructs a doorway of poetry articulating a more integrated life capable of holding in place the mystery and drama of personal suffering. For whatever reason, the individual ends up by needing the Church. And so the young man comes nearer to it.

Before the young man can enter the building, his emotional turmoil must be drawn out like a splinter from infected flesh.

For the time being, only his own drama and his own cycle of life mean anything to him. Other needs go unnoticed. But the ancient wisdom of the Church has always seen that love begins with individual self-love, and only when that all important need is met can the person begin to look out for others. To confront one's own incongruities with truth is the beginning of self-knowledge upon which all further spiritual progress is built.

The instinct for life, especially when it is channeled into a clear choice between growth and destruction, propels the man into the atrium. The contest of the crucible wherein the difficult choice is made is itself the grace of God. The young man enters the building and by doing so, makes an unequivocal choice for life. But how deep will the conversion proceed? The gifts of God—how will they be developed? And will they lead to any real transformation of the individual? The atrium, with all its amusements, represents the difficult phase of purification of desire. Our subject meets with delights and distractions of every sort. The atrium can become very comfortable, just another home like the one he left. Only increasing awareness of the atrium as an architectural introduction to the building proper will allow the person to make his way to the doors of the hall and the awful challenge that awaits him there. Once again, he must encounter life and death, this time not his own, but the life of the Beloved, the Christ, who appears on the cross for his sake and the sake of everyone. Just as before, it is love and life which he chooses. The passion of Christ once seen in its gratuitous and vulnerable form provides him with the power to enter the building through one of the doors. But he has been able to make this choice and answer this summons only because he has been able to apply an ascesis to the distractions of the atrium. And this ascesis has furthered his self-knowledge and awareness of others around him. He sees who is foolish and who is wise, and he throws in his lot with those who enter one of the doors. Meditation on the passion of Christ, and a new knowledge of his own unworthiness are gifts of the Spirit at work in our subject. They bring to a head the dilemma that there are two ways and only two ways. And these ways are diametrically opposed. To ignore Christ is to tread on his blood. To know him is to follow his lead into the building. There is no neutral stance. There is only the way to life and the way to death. The move into the hall can be accomplished only by the transition from the gifts of ascesis and self-knowledge to the acceptance of faith where faith is seen as a participation in the life of God. The young man believes in Christ and moves, that is, changes his life because of this belief. What was heretofore unable to be done is now quite possible because his will, that part of him that lies hidden beneath the surface of conflicting attractions, has been activated by the sanctifying grace of God. The move into the hall, therefore, shows the relationship between the gifts of the Spirit, as aids to the life of faith, and faith itself as a participation in the life of Christ. The gifts are inspirations, observances, techniques and all manner of activities and attitudes designed to open the heart to God's action. But only God can move into the heart in such a way as to enable that heart to meet God where God has chosen to come. This lift off from inspiration to true action is the key to the understanding of growth in the spiritual life.

Inside the Hall

The teeming images of the heavenly liturgy inside the hall serve to describe the plethora of spiritual experiences and our responses to them. In the beginning, grace often acts upon a person in the way of an avalanche which at once overwhelms and forever qualifies the individual. Only time and reflection upon the event can clarify the experience and translate it into concepts about God and actions for God. At first the person is lifted up by undifferentiated feelings of grandeur which affect the senses and also inspire the mind. But almost immediately, the person feels an unworthiness as a sort of reality check upon the experience. When after a bit, one's eyes become accustomed to the place and one is able to begin to see clearly the assembly and the hall, reflection is possible and time must be given to it. This explains the alteration between hearing the word of God in the assembly and the dark pauses for reflection when all the groups of beings digest the Word of God in prayer. The constant return to and fro between time together and time apart becomes the norm for Christian liturgy. Only within this rhythm can the full impact of what has happened in the sacraments be absorbed.

Somewhere during this event of the heavenly liturgy, our subject ceases to be just an individual and becomes part of one of the groups. Now he is a member of Christ's body, a member in such a way as to continue to make progress into the unknown realm of faith. This process of belonging is based on the dialectic of the inner world of spiritual growth and the outer world of Christian liturgy. It is accomplished by means of the Three Degrees of Truth, first formulated by St. Bernard in the twelfth century. An ever-increasing self-knowledge of my issues, that is, my shadows and my sinful patterns, gradually gives way to a concomitant knowledge and appreciation of my neighbor's situation, which I presume must be similar to my own. Thus, knowledge and an inchoate compassion on myself naturally leads to an understanding and compassion of and toward my neighbor. The move to compassion takes sovereign place here, lancing the boils of my own jealousy and envy, and calming my own fears and worries about the aggression of my neighbor. Suddenly, I can be at peace with myself because my fears about my neighbor have been dissolved. I can now afford to go out of my own castle without fretting over who will defend it while I am away. I can leave in order to meet the other person without fear of any advantage the other might take of me. Ironically, my own castle grows and prospers even while I am away. At this point in the process, I begin to notice the Lamb in the center, the Truth in itself. Knowing my own truth and that of my neighbor, I can now view for the first time the ultimate Truth as it is in itself. Worship takes on new dimensions. Anything I thought I was giving of myself in my compassion towards my neighbor I now receive back many times over as I worship the Lamb and as the light and warmth of his divinity play over me. I become aware of the person of the Word, his incarnation and the human instruments by which he came to us. Their flesh which beheld him first is still the best filter for our eyes to see him, as the theology of the East constantly proclaims in their churches. Yet, in the sacrament, he is revealed to the heart without mediation. Still, the heart must grow in its capacity to receive him. Only the constant application of the Spirit's gifts in the hearing and doing of the word can open the heart to move from graces momentarily received to true and lasting growth in God's own life. This is the true content of faith.

The Color of Their Garments

The groupings of beings show how they have received the theological virtue of faith by the colors of their garments. These not only identify their place in the Church, but also their reception of that designation. As the sacraments feed them with the life of God, their activity in the Church increases. Their song grows fuller and their garments grow richer in color because of the gifts of the Spirit which exercise their hearts. So the interchange between the promptings of the Spirit and the growth in the content of their faith result in the holiness of their lives. The various colors exhibited in the assembly demonstrate the complexity of God's life among his people, with all their diverse roles and occupations. His revelation spreads throughout the human spectrum to include the married, the unmarried, the vowed and the non-vowed, the professional and the laborer, the professional religious and the lay person. All are called to holiness, because all are taught by God. None was rejected by Jesus in his public ministry. We can delve further into this mystery by considering the apparent washout of color in the assembly where the monastics are found.

The monastics seem pale in comparison with the others. They are positioned in the places under the windows with clear glass. If the sun should ever move past these windows, the monastics would have to take it full in the face. And, in fact, this happens at one point during the heavenly liturgy. All had to shield their eyes when the uncircumscribed light pierced the hall. What does the paleness and neglect of light signify? And will it indicate what the explosion of light might mean?

The paleness of their robes indicates the quieting of apostolic activity among the monastics. It is to be assumed that, while their gifts were being developed and the spiritual life was growing in content, their robes had enjoyed a deeper hue. But now, a deeper action of God's has begun to empty out their former richness. We may call it the movement into hope, where a purification must occur on the way to love. The middle chapters of this book will describe what the monastics do during the heavenly liturgy, and what God does to them. We can relate what happens in a few lines of print. But what it means would take more books than could be written.

The richness of the monastic tradition took centuries to mature. All the possible applications of the virtues of faith, hope and love to every possible variation in culture, human ability and variety have resulted in charisms of incredible versatility. The monastic tradition has seen and done almost everything in its long history. Its most lasting achievement, however, has been to chart the royal way of holiness for the entire Church. When others were busy preaching the gospel to foreign lands and building up the fabric of social concern in the West, the monastics remained hidden in their cloisters, living the gospel among themselves in controlled conditions, as they had been called to do. Even where a legitimate apostolic activity was adopted, there was still the protection of the community and the stability of the individuals around that nucleus. This intentional atmosphere allowed them the freedom to develop the full use of the gifts of the Spirit for the sake of growth in the life of God, that is, in faith, hope and love.

The monastics, in fact, took the theology of St. Paul in the First Letter to the Corinthians at chapters twelve to fourteen quite seriously. They saw that no matter how gracious and numerous the gifts of the Spirit were, including the monastic charism, their most important and only real result is faith moving to hope and gradually to love. Love is last, as the hymn to love in the thirteenth chapter shows. For who can live this infinitely generous form of patience and charity? Only one who has plumbed the depths of the gospel and who has there found and put on the very life of Christ, so that one no longer lives, but rather, Christ lives within them.The handing over of my life to God is so that Christ may start to live his risen life in me. And the search for this deeper love is worth all the energy and pursuit that the generosity of the human spirit can give. It took the monastic tradition centuries to find the ways best suited to pursue this love and to possess it. The task is well documented in the writings of the holy ones through the centuries. It is incumbent upon monastics today to preserve the knowledge of this pursuit for others in the Church. They must not only save it, but explain it in a language which people of our time can understand.

The Classic Three Stages

The living of the gospel can be put on gradually like a garment. But it has its own internal order and structure. This structure has been best described in three stages which the tradition has identified and never wavered from, although there are differences in the accidentals of it. These are faith, hope and love, or the stages of striving, proceeding and possession, or the stages of purgation, progress and union. They are not mere descriptions of the life of God acting in the person, but are guideposts on the way to a complete identification with God. For these three virtues or stages have as their goal the transformation of the human person into Christ. While they are always active in whatever order in the life of grace by the reception of the sacraments and virtuous living, they are only transformational, that is, fully effective in their proper order. A person may live for long years in the realm of faith before moving slowly on to hope and love. While it is possible to slip out of one of these stages back below to the introductory stages, it is more than likely that God will preserve one in full faith and move that person onto hope and to love, according to his good pleasure. First is faith, when, after a certain discipline and observance of rules, the person begins to accept the first participation in the life of God. This faith is never achieved without living through the *dura et aspera* of the spiritual journey. Here, all the waywardness of the human heart must be confronted and expelled, at least to the point where a certain constancy can be lived. God, who is never compelled to act upon us, waits until the soil of the heart is plowed enough for him to plant his seed, and for the subsequent grain to spring up and grow into food for others.

The terrain of faith is wide and broad, with many varied features in the landscape. Here, the outward apostolic life flourishes, gifts of preaching and teaching are perfected, the moral life is deepened as all the disparate elements of the heart gradually coalesce into a single focus of commitment. When the seed of faith has been sufficiently matured, and when the human person has lived all its effects for the time that God judges to be fitting, then God begins to act further on the person by testing one's resolve by the withdrawal of consolation or by the emptying out of gifts, or if not the emptying, then the removal of the reward from them that one formerly enjoyed. Jesus described this journey from faith to hope very frequently in his teaching. The Lukan Beatitudes (Lk 6:20-26) can serve as an example. After one has practiced poverty to the point of a mature discipline, and after one has learned to live with severe constraints of the three primaries, sex, food and sleep, and after one has learned to confront one's own sins and to weep for them, there remains the last test, the ability to live with persecution even for being good. God seems to darken the path, to take away that which we had gotten used to. God makes us seem a stranger even in our own church or community. Jesus' teaching is abundantly clear. One cannot avoid the Cross of rejection if one is to traverse this terrain of faith, moving to hope and to love. Life becomes wan and pale. The desert, now not of merely human supports as at the beginning, takes on the ghastly feeling of the absence of God, or, at least the *absence* of God's presence. A certain paralysis seems to take over one's life. Tensions reappear which once were thought to have been resolved. The cycle seems to start all over again. One has only faith, and faith is kept alive only by eschatological hope in the final victory of goodness and love. The heart groans with the burden of longing for the full revelation of God not just in one's own heart, but more so in the world. One feels the tension in all creation and in every upright person for the peaceful reign of goodness. But in the here and now, rejection and pain seem to have been the victors.

It is at this point on the journey when a hidden apostolic fruitfulness becomes active. The person cannot see it or experience it. Yet faith insists that the person has become the instrument of God's approach to many hearts in the world. Once a passageway has been cleared into the depths of any human heart, God's love and action are more apparent, and are more easily available to those who are striving earlier on the way.

Now we are close to what the ancients called purity of heart, *apatheia* or self-mastery (*maitrise de soi*). Here God has complete sway over the human person in the clarity of *theoria* or contemplation. Here, the human person is passive to God's sovereign action. No human obstructions can now prevent the almost total transformation into Christ. Here, too, there is no dichotomy between love of neighbor and the love of God. Formerly, while still on the way, it seemed to many monastics that the love of God in contemplation was interrupted by the descent to fraternal charity. Now that fallacy, as inevitably as it seems to intrude itself, falls away and the clear passage to new love of the world cannot be separated from the total love of God. Here is Jesus' willingness to become sin so that we might be saved. Here is St. Paul's declaration that he would rather be separated from Christ than that one should be lost. Here, the love of Christ in a place apart passes into love of Christ wherever he goes in his paschal fullness. As Lord of the cosmos, he takes with him his truest lovers in a freedom not to be guessed at and never to be intuited, only longed for and desired.

The Shadow and its Meaning

What is the case for individuals as they pass from faith to hope and love seems to have happened to the monastics as a group. Having completed the charting of the journey of gospel living through striving, proceeding and possession, they have fallen silent as the energy of the Spirit moves elsewhere in the Church. Many of the gifts have been withdrawn, though the treasury of what has been garnered will always remain intact. Their robes have been washed pale in their suffering. They wait to see what God will do, as their numbers dwindle, as their identity in a revitalized Church comes into question, and as they move painfully through the longing of the final revelation of the children of God.

With the proclamation of the documents of the Vatican Council, there was a sense that all was ready for a new and major shift. There was so much that had been completed, so much of the past had already been preserved and studied thanks to the gifts of scientific history. When it was time to move forward in and during the council, suddenly there was nowhere to go for many of the religious. The monastics seemed to be the most secure, because of their long tradition. But when the full implications of the universal call to holiness of *Lumen Gentium* began to be felt, the larger questions and the greater challenge dawned on the monastics only slowly. And on many it has not even yet become apparent. For the monastic way is no longer the only way to holiness, and it is not even the surest way, now that the Spirit is moving among the other groups gathered at the heavenly liturgy. Where then is our unique place, as others learn to live the gospel in the workplace using our own tools? Where are the bishops who will understand this shift and know how to include us in a new ecclesiology that stands poised to sanctify the world? How will a closer collaboration with the Church under the guidance of the bishops come about, when we insist blindly to follow the grace of our founders who knew a quite different Church? How should this statement from the council be interpreted, even when the same council told us that we are to reform and update our lives to the modern (postmodern) world?

There is also the sense that, at the time of the council, not only was everything ready, but it was overripe. The Church had for too long been turned in on itself, while the cultures of the world, having suffered the appalling disasters of two world wars, numerous genocides and the Holocaust, were moving on to a more explicit embrace of the information explosion which shows no sign of slowing. Can we not say that the Spirit has already seen the Church's need to evangelize the new world order by sending out the baptized newly equipped with the Spirit's own gifts of holiness garnered from the treasure house of the past? Can we not discern the Spirit's major shift in the Church from preserving and maintaining old institutes to inspiring and nurturing new groups to complete God's revelation in the married and in the professional people of the world? Can the Spirit redraw the lines separating the sacred and the profane? Is this not what the council tried to do? How blasphemous then, when groups in the Church try to stop this movement by returning to old models of brittle observance and dried, shredded concepts. How small the faith of these endeavors. What an inversion of the Spirit's gifts. What a heresy! How unfaithful to the legacy of Gregory the Great, who refused to listen to the voices of doom that said that the West would descend into chaos, and moved instead to send missionaries to a new world! How different history would have been without that move of the Spirit or the holiness of that monk-pope's life.

The Place to be Loved

The Church of the Vatican Council has turned toward the world waiting to be saved. The Church stands equipped with a glorious spiritual tradition that needs to be shared. It is up to the monastics to reinterpret that tradition and to share it with the Church so that the Church may share it with the world. We are now ready to give the color of our robes to others. Indeed, from time to time, the pure light of God will shine upon us to indicate the glory that awaits those who live in blind faith, transparent hope and unfelt love. Like Jesus transfigured on the mountain, the monastics wait for this uncircumscribed light to fall from heaven in order to teach our followers the heights and the depths of the calling. But then, wounded and veiled like Moses, we come down from the mountain of light to take up again the emptiness and dreariness of despoiled communities and the fraternity of weakness.

The glory of development, the growth in holiness and the fuller experience of the Spirit's gifts goes now to others in the Church. The "place" of encounter with Christ has started to move from the inner places of protection to the outer places of risk where the Spirit waits on the ramparts to sanctify the world. What will the world become, if the baptized begin to act as the leaven of Christ's life in its very midst? As faith, hope and love spread to more and more people, what will the encounter between East and West come to mean? As the glory of God moves into the center of the world, will the children of God, north and south, know a new justice? Will the creation, groaning in travail, sustain us into the third millennium? These questions, as large as they seem, take on a new urgency if we interpret the Vatican Council with courage and a sure sense of the spiritual tradition from which we have come. There are only two ways. There is no way in between the right and the wrong. There is no way free of risk. We must either have trust in the Church to go forward, or perish by betraying the Spirit.

CHAPTER THREE

Within the Gates:
The Monastic Gifts

The gifts we speak of in this chapter are the tools, the instruments and the techniques which monastics use in order to put on Christ and to know his power and love. They are gifts because they come from God's own Spirit, working in the world and ordering the customs and habits of people who long to move forward on the spiritual journey. Except for the Eucharist and the *Opus Dei* (the Liturgy of the Hours), the gifts are not ends in themselves, of course; they are not worship or liturgy. They can be changed, altered or developed from place to place and from time to time to fit the circumstances of cultures and epochs, climates and regions. There is no greater testimony to the presence and action of the risen Christ in the world than that his spirit should inspire men and women of every place and time to do those works which will open their hearts to receive God's greater gift of his own life in the virtues of faith, hope and love.

For the devout person the Eucharist as the source and summit of the Christian life is already in place even before the adoption of the monastic charism. To discuss the Eucharist and the Liturgy of the Hours as part of monastic prayer and worship, and to position them after a discussion of primary ascesis does not relegate them to an inferior place in the monastic life. Rather it implies that they have brought the Christian to the place where a more focused and interiorized life may begin. Once that monastic journey has begun, different attitudes and dispositions are brought to bear on the celebration of both the Liturgy of the Hours and the Eucharist. The Eucharist then has already done its work as source. It remains to be seen how it will unfold as summit.

The monastic practices included here are gleaned from the tradition of the Rule of St. Benedict, especially at chapter four, "The Instruments of Good Works." There, St. Benedict provides seventy-two short statements about discipline and behavior. Here, we propose only seven elements of observance as a summary of the spirituality contained in chapter four of St. Benedict's Rule. By doing so, we hope to encapsulate and condense. But we also anticipate the needs of persons who are just starting out on the monastic way in a monastery, and more especially, those who would like to inculcate the monastic tradition into their lives outside the monastery and in the wider Church. The order of the gifts presented here, therefore, is existential in nature, beginning with first practices which the Spirit seems to suggest to persons, and continuing on with the series according to the experience of the spiritually mature.

The First Gift: Primary Ascesis

Sex, Food and Sleep

The three primaries touch on the necessities of life itself. We cannot live without these bodily realities. They need to be met each day in some form. By taking into control these primaries, the ascetic person strives to reveal, evaluate and adjust what our culture says about these needs. For example, if our secular culture prides itself on the liberation from sexual constraints, how do people who choose to adhere to a traditional Christian morality articulate and honor such an ideal in an indifferent or even hostile climate? In the case of nourishment, we, in the first and second worlds, take for absolute granted our nourishment, without even a thought to constraint as to taste and amount. Only the health conscious and the diet watchers have successfully introduced a curb on the appetite for taste and indulgence of food. Again, our culture presumes a complete night's rest and rarely imposes a fast from sleep.

We are too afraid of the consequences: grumpiness, ill humor, nervousness and gnawing fatigue.

But universal religious tradition has always taught that if you want to monitor the spiritual journey, you must begin with the body and the control of its appetites, especially the necessities. In the Christian tradition, there is no awakening of the spiritual realities without a concomitant response in the body. We are both exterior body and interior person. Our personhood cannot be divided. If, as it is stated in the Letter of James, you cannot have faith without showing some evidence of it in good works done to a neighbor, so also you cannot have authentic spiritual growth without some exercise of control over the instinctual needs of the body. Therefore, we cannot retreat from basic ascetic practice, but we must re-image it for our own time which is unsympathetic to it.

The Christian tradition has often been accused of imbalance when it comes to ascetical practice. Some saints have performed astounding feats of self-denial, thereby seeming to exalt a body-hating attitude worthy of Plotinus. But this unfortunate tendency to exaggeration is easily exposed when less motivated people try to overdo ascetical practices with disastrous results. "Thus you will know them by their fruits" (Matt 7:20). There is nothing which God has created that is not good and beautiful. Jesus himself declared all foods clean when he taught that whatever goes into a person from outside cannot defile. "Rather, it is what comes out of a person that defiles" (Mark 7:17-19). We employ a healthy ascesis, not to deny God's goodness and love, not to suggest that this or that food is unfit or unclean, but to bring the body under control so that it may cooperate with the whole person in doing good.

Why does the monastic tradition insist so heavily on fasting from the necessities of sex, food and sleep? The answer can be found, as is always the case in this tradition, in the gospel itself. Jesus asks how friends of the bridegroom can fast when he is still with them (Matt 9:14-17). And the response is, of course, that they cannot. But Christ has risen, and has gone before us into the whole world, beckoning us on to follow him to the final revelation of the Kingdom. He has gone on before us, therefore, and is not with us in the same way as he was in

Galilee. His Spirit now dwells within us and dictates to Christian monastics that fasting from bodily appetites is salutary, though always secondary to the goal of the gospel itself, namely, the love of God in Christ.

Sexual Restraint

The sexual drive is a relational drive, demanding that the human person should not live alone (see Gen 2:18). Yet, the Christian is a temple of the Holy Spirit, and as such, preserves the body as the inviolate sacred place where only those who are admitted in loving and sacramental commitment can enter. All Christians are called to uplift their sexuality to higher and more comprehensive relational meaning. But the sexual drive can only be channeled into higher levels by the Spirit's power. To ignore it, or to deny it, is to court disaster precisely because one is dallying with untruth. Sexual ascesis, therefore, has two simple goals.

The first is to direct our sexual energy into Christ-filled relationships. Some of these will be in the sacramental marriage state, where the love of the two brings them closer to Christ and his Church. For such as these, for whom marriage is a vocation, it is only in their fidelity to and love for each other that they can put on Christ. Married or not, however, all Christians are called to direct the basic instinctual genital drive to love and service of our neighbor. For monastics, in particular, Jesus' caution about celibacy needs to be held uppermost in the mind, namely, that celibacy is a grace. Since it is a gift, it cannot be won, bargained for or otherwise controlled. Only in prayer and in the loving support of a community of like-minded persons can the monastic hope to live a healthy, sexually responsible life without genital fulfillment.

The second goal, as the monastic tradition constantly reminds us, is to re-image our sexual drive into the love of Christ, where the putting on of the body of Christ, that is, the Church, takes on nuptial significance. This is to imitate Jesus, who, St. Paul tells us, loved the Church and gave himself up for her in a nuptial gesture (see Eph 5:25). Union with the person of Christ in all things, even the imagination, and especially the sexual one, is an elevated goal, but it is implied by the gospels, and encouraged by the theology of St. Paul, who experienced the love of Christ as worth more than life itself. Using the sexual drive as an ally to as full as possible participation in the life of God in faith, hope and love, is to explore the very limits of the human personality as we know it. It is a goal that has been neglected in our time, because it has been deemed impossible or unhealthy by a necessary and long overdue emphasis on the first goal. But with the renewal of the love of the partners in Christian marriage since the Vatican Council, we can hope that the elevation and use of sexuality can be every Christian's goal. Once this is in place, the second goal of complete transformation in Christ can be built on top of it.

Food

Most religious traditions accept the concept of fasting as an aid to the spiritual endeavor. Several comments may be helpful to posit fasting in the context of the spiritual journey we seek to illustrate in this book. By the ordering of bodily appetites and desires, fasting puts a window on the soul of the person. Not so occupied in the mind about food and drink, the person has an opportunity to look inward at the drives and compulsions of the heart. These are much more difficult to control and are the subject of further discussion. For the moment, we must point out some principles of fasting and abstinence.

St. Benedict recommends that the community not direct the amount of food to be taken, except in the most general way (RB 40.1-2). The individual, therefore, must choose what is the most helpful amount of food to be taken. The time of day when food is taken is also important, if it can be so controlled as in a monastery. If we eat only when hungry, we rely too much on the mechanism of the body, which never can have enough or is never tired of making suggestions as to food. The discipline of scheduled meals, whether we are hungry or not, is always beneficial for the overall use of this practice. The abstinence from certain foods forces one to curb specific cravings and adopt constraints on tastes. These observances yield the utmost profit for control of the thoughts, especially sexual images and feelings of envy, anger and melancholy. A diet which is never controlled or rarely curbed is an open invitation to many uncontrollable activities in the mind. In this regard, sameness of alimentary intake, while distasteful on occasion and downright impossible if overdone, gives sweetness and equilibrium to heart and mind. Many monasteries find that a routine breakfast, as well as a third uncooked meal, whether at dinner or supper, leaves the variety to the main meal only. This fosters a good balance between sameness and healthy pleasure in meals.

Obvious care must be taken in order to avoid any abuse of fasting, which injures the peace and harmony of the heart by introducing impossible demands on the physical mechanism. The stories of saints ruining their health by fasting and abstinence are of dubious value. St. Paul's dictum of knowing how to go hungry and how to be filled seems to be sober advice to any one adopting the practice of fasting (see Phil 4:12).

Contemporary dietary practices aimed at low-fat intake and high protein from grains should be welcomed as a workable addition to a spiritual regime. When treated with love and respect, the body is always a willing partner to the practices of prayer and meditation in whatever form they may take during the day. A healthy and well-balanced lifestyle is always the foundation of a strong spiritual life lived over a long period of time. In fact, a strong constitution is almost necessary to receive the further gifts of the Spirit mentioned below, to say nothing of the approach of God in contemplation.

Sleep

Spiritual practice is not a thing of the moment, at one's convenience or whim. It is all or nothing in a person's life. It must be present, therefore, even in one's sleeping habits. For the goal of spiritual practice can be said to be the transformation of consciousness. We seek to regulate that dulling of consciousness, even though it be necessary, which is sleep. An indulgent heart, softened by much sleep, can have no grasp of spiritual intuitions should they enter. They will be misinterpreted or neglected by a slothful mind full of sleep. As with food, the daily discipline of sleep is most helpful. Retirement at the same time, as well as rising, is the best approach to sleep. This is a constant in monastic tradition.

The regulation of sleep yields different modes of energy and consciousness. The Trappist practice of Vigils in the middle of the night, when rising at 3:00 A.M. means the beginning of the day, introduces easy access to the psyche during the hours before dawn. Visual blindness aids concentration on the Psalter, meditation and especially *lectio divina*. With the Scriptures, the mind can roam free in the imagination and allow God's word to have maximum effect. The word enters our dreams and images more easily at the time before the sun's light. The value of this pre-dawn time is revealed when, at the rising of the sun, a new kind of energy is observed and new awaking of consciousness to duties and work. Only in the darkness are certain, more choice intuitions of God received. Early retirement, too, soon after the sun goes down, prepares one to reenter the cycle of prayer in the dark before morning.

A well-regulated timetable allows one to sleep better when it is time to retire. It minimizes the tendency to waste time during the day, and makes all the more precious the gift of time which God has given us.

The Second Gift: Prayer

Hand in hand with the control of the body goes the practice of prayer. In monasteries, prayer is well disciplined in a balance between public prayer, that is, in community, and private devotion. In a deeper sense, it is a way of life made up of different kinds of prayer forms which work together to ready the heart for the prayer which the Spirit offers there to God in Christ.

Lectio Divina

This practice of meditative reading of the Scriptures or other holy writings holds pride of place in the monastic tradition. Not a study, nor a utilitarian reading, it focuses on the entry into the heart of the Word of God with all the power of the Spirit. It is a sacramental time, full of the presence of God through his word. As such, it is the most important prayer time of the day. What is learned there is brought to the community prayer, and what is brought back to *lectio divina* from other types of prayer and the day's activities is more grist for the mill. The alternation between *lectio divina* and its application in one's daily life is perhaps the most profitable and characteristic rhythm of the monastic tradition. This alternation of the Word of God with a life lived in God holds the secret of monastic prayer. For it is not in long hours of pensive meditation that we break through to God, but it is in the natural rhythms of the day and of the psyche and the body that God's approach to us is discerned, approved and welcomed. God moves in and out of our activities. In *lectio divina*, we are more likely to appreciate how God has come to us, even when we were not aware of it, or were too preoccupied with other feelings and motives to discern him. *Lectio divina* never allows us to bathe in our own unrelated sweet thoughts, but always brings us back to God's prophetic word and his saving will in our lives. It resists all attempts at control and prediction of what God may want of us. It refuses the dominance of the mind in formal exegesis, which is necessary in its own time and place. It invites us only to take the journey of ever-increasing digestion of God's holy will for ourselves and the world. It makes real in us the work of Christ in his paschal mystery, which, in the tradition of the ancients, is present on every page of the Bible. *Lectio divina*, therefore, demands a certain traditional Christocentric interpretation of the Scriptures, designed to further in us the theology of the paschal mystery, the dying and the rising to new life of the One who loves us. It keeps constantly in mind the unique focus of the Word of God which is Christ, and which is always theological in this strictest sense. It cries out this and this only, before revealing anything else: "The time is fulfilled, and the kingdom of God has come near; repent and believe in the good news" (Mark 1:15).

Opus Dei

The *Opus Dei*, St. Benedict's term for the Liturgy of the Hours, is the public counterpart of *lectio divina*. The public chanting of the Psalter gathers together the community and the thoughts of all the individuals so as to focus their minds and hearts on the paschal mystery. Here again, the interpretation of the Psalter is a Christocentric one. The Psalter, in psalm after psalm, presents the struggle between Christ, the just one, and the reprobate, the evil one. In this cosmic struggle for justice, which has already been won by Christ, but which continues in his body, the Church, the monastics position their own battles. Here, they receive confirmation of what they have achieved. They acknowledge their own failures and frustrations. They cast their untamable thoughts onto the rock which is Christ and gain strength, in the solace of the community, to go on in confidence. They listen together to the Word of God which directs the community according to God's will. At the end of each Office, in keeping with St. Benedict's explicit precept, they chant the Our Father, and take to heart the phrase, "Forgive us our sins, as we forgive those who trespass against us" (RB 13.12-14). In this way, they blot out any scandal which may have arisen since the last Office, due to lack of charity or failure of communication among the members of the community. It is clear from this injunction that St. Benedict has in mind the preservation of communal calm and the guarantee of continued personal prayer among the brothers.

Meditation

Meditation is a necessary adjunct to the previous two kinds of prayer. There is a kind of meditation that is included in *lectio divina*. One also may use what is called discursive meditation whereby a scene from the life of Christ is the object of one's thoughts for a set period of time. But what we have in mind here, after *lectio divina* and the *Opus Dei*, is a fixed time of imageless, pure prayer, if the individual can face such emptiness. St. Benedict counsels that if this kind of prayer is practiced by the whole community, for example, at the end of an Office, it should be brief (RB 20.5). If it is the custom to include meditation after the chanting of a psalm, as we see outlined in Cassian's *Institutes*, Book 1, then the community regulates the posture and the time. But if it is left to one's own schedule or discipline, then it should have the following elements: a fixed time, perhaps thirty minutes in the morning and fifteen minutes in the evening, or something similar; a fixed posture, either sitting in a kind of lotus position, or sitting on a straight backed chair, or kneeling. Many monastics practice this meditation before the Blessed Sacrament. The necessity of clear, untrammeled consciousness is obvious for this kind of prayer. A spiritual director may help to clarify some of the thoughts that arise during this type of prayer. One should not take fright at the content of such thoughts or of the seeming lack of control of them. The ancients have charted the relationship between the recesses of the heart and the attempts to open the heart to God's action and presence. It should come as no surprise then that many persons leave off imageless meditation when their thoughts will not permit them to continue in peace. For others, it is the sheer boredom that forces them to give up. Here again, a spiritual director may be able to point out to them why God chooses to remain silent, or what the obstacles in one's life may be to a deeper living of the gospel. Whatever the true state of a person's stance is before God, it will become manifest at the time of meditation. For many contemporary people, the Centering Prayer movement helps to structure such meditation. Meditation, however, must be returned to the larger field of *lectio divina*, the *Opus Dei*, and yet even other kinds of prayer, if it is to be the true work of Christ in the individual and if it is therefore to be part of the monastic tradition.

The simple prayer of the heart follows naturally upon the progress of *lectio divina,* the *Opus Dei* and meditation. During all the activities of the day, the thought of God and his Christ come easily when there is a moment to catch one's breath, or in a space of some leisure. Sometimes it is good to structure such remembrances of God during one's work time with ejaculatory prayer or the repetition of some holy phrase such as the Jesus Prayer. The Russian tradition has built a whole system of heart purification on this discipline. Work activity, congenial to simple prayer, without much effort of the mind, has been preferred by monasteries, but even there, it is often impossible to provide for it. Intense, mental activity at work time, which seems to be the lot of modern monastics, can be intentionally broken in order to allow for a moment of quiet and memory. Those outside the monastery should take heart that the love of God, exercised in formal times of prayer, can continue unabated like a low fire, even when the mind is occupied. This same love can grow again to full blaze at the next formal prayer time or at any quiet moment of memory. Even at night, the prayer of simple regard may continue, so that the Scripture may be fulfilled, "I slept but my heart was awake" (Cant 5:2).

The combination of all of the above constitutes a teaching on prayer that has come to be regarded as the quest for continual prayer, or the prayer of the heart. Mentioned several times in the Christian Testament (for example, Luke 18:1; 1 Thess 5:17; Rom 12:12; Eph 6:18; 2 Thess 1:11), and alluded to there in countless other places, it is the stance which allows God free rein to bestow on the person his own virtues of faith, hope and love. It contains within itself a further teaching on the blessedness of creation, and its transparency to the movement of God, since for the pure of heart, everything is pure (Titus 1:15). Further, it demonstrates the absolute need for discernment of what should be allowed in of all the gifts of creation, and what, for the sake of the kingdom, should be left out for my particular journey. It guarantees the sovereignty of God in my life by concentrating consciousness on God and not on myself, thus helping to cancel the unfortunate narcissistic tendencies of the day. As such, it reestablishes God's sway over the world and removes the tendency to blaspheme the Creator and Redeemer of the world.

The Third Gift: The Monastic Way of Worship

The *Opus Dei* is not only an exercise in continual prayer, it is primarily the praise of God in the mystery of the heavenly liturgy. For when the believing community is gathered by the Holy Spirit, and taught by the Spirit's gifts to live in charity and humility with one another and thus forming a particular monastic church, the Liturgy of the Hours makes present and acting the saving mystery of Christ. Through the pascal mystery, which we believe is now present in the worshipping community, this same community becomes part of the heavenly liturgy, such as it is described in the Book of Revelation in chapters four and five. There, the Lamb that was slain draws all to himself and thus offers the acceptable sacrifice to God. In, through and with Christ, we can offer worthy praise to God, and by means of Christ, all creation joins in the rejoicing. It is the privilege of those monastics who, fixed in stability in their community, and who enjoy a certain exemption from any particular church with no or very limited apostolic activity, to share in the concern and ministry of every church throughout the world. But it is also their privilege to join the local Church under the presidency of its bishop in all its joys and sorrows and thus to complete the image of the Church in each locality as it preaches the Word and prays to the Father in Christ. From the periphery of any Church, the monastic Church reaches to the center, and there, in purity of heart, the monastics enter into the collective heart of humanity and monitor and pray for its struggle for the light.

The Eucharist is our foretaste of the heavenly liturgy in a preeminent way. For the monastic community, the Sunday Eucharist takes on special significance, even as it also does in all the local churches. For with the Sunday liturgy, with its attendant first and second vespers, the Word of God is broken open with special solemnity according to the riches of the lectionary. The Eucharist thus fosters a unique encounter with Christ through the mystery of the particular teaching contained in the Word of God for that celebration. The monastics also build their *lectio divina* around that teaching with additional time on Sunday consecrated to it. The monastic community forms itself around the enfolding cycle of the liturgical year. The ring of Christ winds its way deeper and deeper into the monastic heart, building up the fruits and gifts of the Spirit according to the monastic tradition, and guiding the monastic along the way of humility until perfect love should cast out all fear. It is in the cycle of the liturgical year, with its constant promotion of the mystery of Christ, that the monastic heart takes on the Christian mystery and gradually becomes conformed to the person of Christ for the sake of one's community and for the sake of the world's wider freedom.

The Fourth Gift: Examen

The monastic may now embark on a more interior journey by means of self-awareness or self-knowledge. The grace of God will invite the person more and more deeply and frequently to enter the depths of the heart, there to discover hidden sources of motives and behavior. God will permit this and foster it only to the extent that the person has received the Spirit's strength to do so. We might also add that God's grace takes the form of psychological fortitude to face the reality of the waywardness of the human heart and all its deception. Parallel to my own self-knowledge goes the understanding of the weakness and failure of others and the general moral weakness of nations and peoples. This knowledge is also accompanied by attempts at transparency with my neighbor and the readiness to ask forgiveness for wrongs committed.

The monastic tradition institutionalizes this examen by frequent, fervent use of the sacrament of reconciliation. If this is not possible, then the use of a spiritual director, who is either the abbot or a trusted senior is usually made. The daily examen at the noonday *Angelus* or after the evening *Salve* brings to mind the need for constant vigilance over the heart and never permits the sun to go down on some unacknowledged sin. Neither does it allow the sinful indulgence of thinking myself holy before I am holy or the even greater sin of a favorable comparison at the expense of my neighbor. The brief, quiet moments of prayer during intense work activity are also the time for a review of one's priorities.

Progress along this road of the examen brings one also to a crossroads and a new insistence on the opposition of the two ways. Once I begin to seek the forgiveness of my neighbor on the way of transparency, which is the way of goodness, light and Truth itself, then I must continue on this way, never hiding anything that wants to come to exposure, and never deliberately obfuscating my intentions and motives. Any retreat from this way forces me not to a standstill of neutrality but to the tortuous and fragmented way—broad and wide—of excommunication self-inflicted.

The Fifth Gift: A Home to Live In

Hand in hand with the knowledge of my unworthiness goes the growing comfort of my interior home. The paradox of healthy sorrow for sin coupled with increasing peace of heart can only be explained by the new ordering of appetites. Somehow we are closer to the Truth, and the human person finds relief and joy. When this interior home is identified and experienced, we go there far more frequently, with less resistance and with quicker steps and longer stays. The content of this peace is not just a narcotic kind of comfort, but the enjoyment of a new sense of self-worth, even as I grow in self-knowledge. Automatically, I experience a new comfort level with others, a new security based on truth. I see less compulsiveness and an easier control over my emotions and actions. All this amounts to a new identity, which is at the same time not new, but rediscovered. Whatever it is, I know that it is built on rock, that my storm and my rising waves cannot sweep it away. That is precisely the reason for my peace. I begin to trust my inner home. I now know at least a measure of "strength of soul."

If I keep examining this new confidence in myself, I realize that it is not so much in myself as it is in God's love for me. Here I discover a deeper center, which I still call home, but which I intuit is bottomless. This neither frightens nor puzzles me. It seems somehow natural to my being, if not to my mind, which is confused by the philosophical and theological implications. Can this be the place where God abides, and where God is content to stay? However I reflect on this mystery, I yearn for its further development, despite myself. I warm to it as a moth to the flame. Or as the fly to the light. I grow silent about it as well, for there seems no adequate way to articulate that deep delight which I feel inside me. I develop a new taste for silence and solitude, which I once so feared or suspected of deceit. I detect more easily my need for this balance in my life, for I instinctively want to protect my interior home. But a heavy responsibility accompanies my growth. For I must carry with me the knowledge of an ignorant and flighty world which cannot see that its tragedy, so bewailed and indulged, is largely avoidable and unnecessary. The content of tragedy, in fact, gets emptied out by the paschal mystery of Jesus, which has already conquered the evil of the world. But we are still left with the mystery of the refusal of the human heart to acknowledge God. This is not so much tragedy as it is stubbornness and stupidity. This knowledge becomes the burden of patience, willingly born by those whose heart God has made his home.

The Sixth Gift: The Cloister

The previous gifts begin to coalesce into a discipline of a new configuration, representing a more inclusive integration of the spiritual person. In the monastery, we are speaking of that maturity which is demanded of those to whom more responsibility is given for longer labors, and even frequent trips outside the enclosure. They must keep alive the discipline of the enclosure, but in ways that permit them to perform the tasks they have been legitimately given outside the monastery. More give and take is required; more flexibility and more creativity in the spiritual craft is demanded, so that no loss of profit may result from the increase in fraternal charity which they are asked to give.

For those outside the monastery, life in this culture of richness, overabundance and instant gratification offers similar challenges with the need perhaps of even greater dedication to the spiritual disciplines already learned. Might we say this is the most difficult step for spiritual people outside the monastery? For how can they construct an interior cloister in this frenzied world of ours? Basing ourselves on the gifts already discussed, we note three areas of concern where the walls of a spiritual enclosure must be built and guarded, not so much to keep the world outside its limits, but to keep the monastic person from wandering about outside unnecessarily.

Body

One must never force the machine of the body to an excess of work or pleasure, because the first thing that suffers is prayer. In fatigue, one loses the dedication to the interior home. One is too exhausted to avoid neglect, and the resulting discouragement may cause damage for a long time to come and lead to a downward spiral that only the mercy of God can slow. The monastic diet must be carefully maintained. Indulgence to the point of illness must always be foreign. Sufficient sleep and a certain amount of body care in the form of exercise or yoga is usually needed to maintain the freshness of the mind. The monastic culture of the West has been painfully slow to develop a good body culture. What was formally achieved by manual chores and farm work has now been left fallow in the lives of many. To be sure, numerous individuals in our monasteries have begun to rectify this imbalance, but we are a long way from conscious monastic articulation of the proper care of the body in a postmodern culture.

Time

The scheduling of activities, adhered to with as much fidelity as possible, signals a new awareness of the sacredness of time. The exercises of prayer, of *lectio divina*, of meditation are so much more fruitful if accorded the same time each day. When this is not possible, as it frequently is not, one must develop a sensitivity to rhythms of fertility, when, for example, it is an appropriate time for prayer, even outside my schedule, or when the need for silence or solitude must take precedence over a supposedly necessary activity. Here one must make choices, maintain barriers and draw limits with the sure hand of the Spirit as guide.

Relationships

No monastic enclosure, no matter how strict, can guard a person against damaging relationships. For even when we are separated from a destructive or profitless person by walls or schedules, the mind can produce longings and yearnings, recriminations and guilt feelings far beyond any reason or rhyme. What one person can give has limits. What might be wasted on an inappropriate meeting can always be preserved.

What is profitable for another is told only in the Spirit. What might be received occurs only in grace and truth.

When demands are made in any of these three areas, a new discernment must be made and, perhaps, new sacrifices. We must be sure of preserving our steadiness along the way. Are there codependent relationships that bind me fast or send me beyond my cloister? Are there situations which hamper my freedom and bring on compulsions to which I cannot say no? Are there choices of career or employment that have led me down a wrong path? Am I powerless to reverse this direction? If my call in the spiritual life is authentic and in Christ, then there is no one preventing me from being a monastic except myself. If I look carefully around me, everything I need is contained within this monastic discipline and within this spiritual enclosure. There is no need to roam around outside looking for salvation when the truth of God's love awaits me inside myself.

The Seventh Gift: Discretion

The gift of discretion tells a person when to push ahead and when to pull back. It knows when to unleash zeal and when to exercise the utmost caution. It also knows when to have mercy on my own weakness. The strength and the weakness of the flesh are always transparent to the person of discretion. When the flesh is fertile by the Spirit and when it is not, discretion knows as well. Such a person can let go the raw energy of power, pent up for long periods, and control it with precision skill, fearing nothing when it is for a just cause. But with the same precision, it knows the sensitivity of others and how quickly another can be hurt. Discretion is ever vigilant. It always has the gospel and the conversion of another at heart. Mindful of its own ways, discretion knows the motives of others because it understands the sources of energy, and it knows when another's energy is inappropriate. It knows who touched it, and for what reason. Because the other stands revealed, discretion knows the proper response for the improper behavior. With evil, it never responds in kind. Where there is ugly force, it blunts. Where there is a harsh tongue, it soothes. Where there is the lack of peace of whatever kind, it brings the restorative balm of irenic reason to bear most patiently. Discretion, in short, finds the Royal Way, looking neither to the right nor to the left. It is therefore not predictable by any formula or measurement. It exercises wisdom, sees the golden where others see the grey, and it pushes forward to the brilliance of Truth wherever Christ chooses to be seen.

• • •

These are the gifts of the monastic spiritual craft. They can be exercised within or without the walls of a monastery. They have a long tradition behind them, but, as with the treasure house of the Church, they can bring forth things new and old in a surprising reconfiguration. They demand only a faithfulness and a love that is both strong and tender, adventuresome and tame, beautiful but hidden. It is Christ that raises up such love, and he alone in his risen body can pass it on to those whom he loves and whom he chooses.

CHAPTER FOUR

The Desert and the Garden:
The Steps of Humility 1–3

The desert is far from the world and, therefore, free of its distractions. Newcomers to the monastic life, however, do not enter into a featureless world, but a society replete with centuries-old structures. Life according to the Rule of St. Benedict (= RB) may be a desert, but it is so only in the experience of the novice. In reality, it is a world of peace, concord, order—a place to love. Knowing full well that the heart is the beast to be tamed, the monastic founders went right to the root of the society's problems and set up monastic structures that would go clean contrary to the patterns of the undisciplined heart. The RB captures this first insightful discipline, and, though it is a sixth-century text, stores up the best vintage of the first monks and nuns. Taming the heart requires a sense of place. It roots not just the mind to a set of principles, but also the body to a piece of land. Each has an important lesson to teach the other. Spiritual doctrine remains in the head and not in the heart, unless it is lived out in time in a given place. Yet the heart has yearnings and wanderings far beyond any place in which we may abide. It is when the heart looks beyond itself that God most frequently responds to it and will even come to dwell there for longer and longer periods. This transfer from the heart as a place of peace and order for me, to a place where God may abide signals the passage from my action to God's action, or from my active life to the contemplative life in God. When the Rule leads to the contemplative life, it is most truly a garden.

The Rule, its sources and its long history of commentators have codified this spiritual passage by the twelve steps of humility in chapter seven. The number "twelve" designates a sacred completeness, so that we could say that this chapter represents a kind of *summa* of monastic living. The steps ascend with intensity and mark guideposts along the journey rather than arrival at any one place. How can this humility be the delight of the garden, when it even lowers the head in remembrance of and sorrow for sin? How can we consider this chapter of the Rule as the awakening to new life after the purgation of the desert? What worldview of any legitimate desire could possibly be built on such an observance or lifestyle? The answer lies in our understanding of how monastic observances work in a person's life. For if we think of these steps as so many observances which can be put on at will, then we are as mistaken as one who speeds through the twelve steps of Alcoholics Anonymous. We do not climb up the ladder; we are drawn up by someone and something that appeals to us from above and beyond. Once we set our foot to this ladder, we cannot help but accept or reject someone or something that is outside the self we can perceive. To help the image of the ladder, we could think of each rung as a room opening onto a larger room, whose windows, showing a different landscape, compel us to explore the door and pass through it. The comparison is not between this world of skewed values and the pure, airy world at the top of the ladder, but between a diminished sense of self glued to the floor of untruth, and the height of the ladder which expands the person to take in more and more reality, a reality redeemed and revealed by Christ as the Truth. The ladder of willing humility then becomes the staircase to richer, fuller living, not in some thing-less, transparent world of philosophical escape outside the house, but to a freedom which breaks down doors in an over organized household, and lights the fire and ensures comfort and truth as God would have it. Our compartmentalized world, and the sterile values in it, are as the daily winter darkness compared to the long sweet late-day sunshine of spring shining in the windows of a liberated home. Once this spring penetrates the bones long accustomed to winter, it revives the shrunken heart, gives suppleness to arthritic limbs and joints, and infuses all with its hope. What started out as the labor of humility, finished with the joy of inspired living. Knowing the truth of our situation, what hope awaits us, and the freedom from the enormous weight of fear, guilt and dreary self-justification, we can experience our life as a garden of delights, where our satisfaction is both within and without. To want to stay on the floor of untruth, with our heads bowed out of habit, with eyes used to looking for lesser life below, seems utter foolishness. Let us proceed then to ascend to life in God by the truth which humility is.

When all the steps have been climbed, St. Benedict promises to the one who perseveres the perfect love that casts out fear. All along the way, God's action on the heart has proceeded apace in the building up of the full content of faith and the consolation of hope. Greater and greater do these grow until at some mysterious point in the latter steps, there is an unqualified surrender of the person to God, perhaps unknown to the conscious mind, but transparent in actions. The rest of the steps fall into place quickly and the person enjoys the freedom and the complete mobility of the new creation.

When we speak of faith, hope and love as not just momentary inspirations of God but as a sharing in the very life of God, then we can equate them with the classic three stages of the spiritual life, that is, striving, proceeding and fulfillment. Furthermore, in the twelve steps of humility, we can trace the gradual build up of faith in steps one, two and three; the painful passage to hope in steps four through seven; and the gradual ascension of love in the heart in steps eight through twelve. This assignment of the various steps to specific places along the journey to contemplation or transformation in Christ is valid when the steps become more or less normative in a person's life, that is, when they become lasting and discernible traits imbedded in the human person. The boundaries separating the groups of steps may be fluid in either direction. But the doctrines and examples used to explain them accentuate the gradual growth that takes place as the steps become real in a person's life.

The Rule of St. Benedict
Chapter Seven: Humility (RB 7.1-9)

Introduction

[1]Brothers, divine Scripture calls to us saying: *Whoever exalts himself shall be humbled, and whoever humbles himself shall be exalted (Luke 14:11; 18:14).* [2]In saying this, therefore, it shows us that every exaltation is a kind of pride, [3]which the Prophet indicates he has shunned, saying: *O Lord, my heart is not exalted; my eyes are not lifted up and I have not walked in the ways of the great nor gone after marvels beyond me* (Ps 130[131]:1). [4]And why? *If I had not a humble spirit, but were exalted instead, then you would treat me like a weaned child on its mother's lap* (Ps 130[131]:2).

[5]Accordingly, brothers, if we want to reach the highest summit of humility, if we desire to attain speedily that exaltation in heaven to which we climb by the humility of this present life, [6]then by our ascending actions we must set up that ladder on which Jacob in a dream saw *angels descending and ascending* (Gen 18:12). [7]Without doubt, this descent and ascent can signify only that we descend by exaltation and ascend by humility. [8]Now the ladder erected is our life on earth, and if we humble our hearts the Lord will raise it to heaven. [9]We may call our body and soul the sides of this ladder, into which our divine vocation has fitted the various steps of humility and discipline as we ascend.[1]

•••

Christ himself taught that the first shall be last and the last first. If we take the last place, Truth counsels, we shall be in-

---

[1] This and all subsequent references to the Rule (including Benedict's scriptural excerpts imbedded in the text) are taken from *RB 1980: The Rule of St. Benedict*, ed. Timothy Fry, O.S.B. (Collegeville, Minn.: The Liturgical Press, 1981).

vited to a higher place which is lasting and beyond any scheming ambition we may have envisioned. The RB codifies this behavior and sets up structures which are the inverse of how most people would behave. St. Bernard, the principal representative of Cistercian spirituality, summed up the Rule in a kind of antithesis to normal societal values:

> We stay in our place, we who have chosen to be counted for nothing in the house of our God, rather than to dwell in the tabernacles of the wicked:
>
> > Our "place" is the lowest;
> >   It is humility,
> >   voluntary poverty,
> >   obedience, peace and joy in the Holy Spirit.
> > Our place is to be under a master,
> >   under an abbot,
> >   under a rule,
> >   and under a discipline.
> > Our place is to cultivate silence,
> >   and to concentrate on
> >   fasts,
> >   vigils,
> >   prayers,
> >   manual work,
> > and, above all, to keep to that more excellent way
> >   which is charity,
> > and what's more, to advance in all these things
> >   day by day,
> > and, until the very last day, to persevere in them still.[2]

Since Christ taught such an impossible doctrine, only with the help of Christ can it be lived. St. Bernard saw this truth when he went to teach the Rule to his twelfth-century monks. In the new monasticism emerging at that time, the monastics longed for the more obvious presence and action of Christ. They wished to speak his name, to picture him in their meditation, to savor his memory at every moment so that their love for him would be a palpable part of their daily lives. St. Bernard

---

[2] *Sancti Bernaradi Opera*, [letter 142] (Roma: Editiones Cistercienses, 1974) vol. VII, *epistola 142*, p. 340, n. 1, lines 11–16.

accommodated them by suggesting that at the top of St. Benedict's ladder Christ stands as *truth*. Christ is looking down to
see who is coming up, and, perceiving that some are discouraged and others are fearful, he hurries down to help them and
to be their "Way." Eventually, some will succeed in coming to
him who himself is the "Life." By using the admirable Johan-
nine phrase, "I am the way, the truth and the life" (John 14:6),
St. Bernard manages to make Christocentric this introductory
paragraph of the Rule and to ensure its attractiveness to his
audience. For Christian monastics of all times this fact comes
home most clearly, that without the constant help of the Savior no such ascent along the ladder of humility is possible. He
is the very *forma mansuetudinis*, the form of humility. It is
Christ who calls those who start on this ladder. He means to
introduce his counter cultural ways into the soul and the body
with a transforming integration. Far from degrading his disciples, Christ intends to give them a new kind of life based on
a deeper truth than that which they normally encounter.

Step One: RB 7.10-30

¹⁰The first step of humility, then, is that a man keeps
the *fear of God* always *before his eyes* (Ps 35[36]:2) and
never forgets it. ¹¹He must constantly remember everything God has commanded, keeping in mind that all
who despise God will burn in hell for their sins, and all
who fear God have everlasting life awaiting them.
¹²While he guards himself at every moment from sins
and vices of thought or tongue, of hand or foot, of self-
will or bodily desire, ¹³let him recall that he is always
seen by God in heaven, that his actions everywhere are
in God's sight and are reported by angels at every hour.

¹⁴The Prophet indicates this to us when he shows that
our thoughts are always present to God, saying: *God who
searches hearts and minds* (Ps 7:10); ¹⁵again he says: *The Lord
knows the thoughts of men* (Ps 93[94]:11); ¹⁶likewise, *From
afar you know my thoughts* (Ps 138[139]:3) ¹⁷and, *The thought
of man shall give you praise* (Ps 75[76]:11). ¹⁸That he may
take care to avoid sinful thoughts, the virtuous brother

must always say to himself: *I shall be blameless in his sight if I guard myself from my own wickedness* (Ps 17[18]:24).

[19]Truly, we are forbidden to do our own will, for Scripture tells us: *Turn away from your desires* (Sir 18:30). [20]And in the Prayer too we ask God that his *will be done* in us (Matt 6:10). [21]We are rightly taught not to do our own will, since we dread what Scripture says: *There are ways which men call right that in the end plunge into the depths of hell* (Prov 16:25). [22]Moreover, we fear what is said of those who ignore this: *They are corrupt and have become depraved in their desires* (Ps 13[14]:1).

[23]As for the desires of the body, we must believe that God is always with us, for *All my desires are known to you* (Ps 37[38]:10), as the Prophet tells the Lord. [24]We must then be on guard against any base desire, because death is stationed near the gateway of pleasure. [25]For this reason Scripture warns us, *Pursue not your lusts* (Sir 18:30).

[26]Accordingly, if *the eyes of the Lord are watching the good and the wicked* (Prov 15:3), [27]if at all times *the Lord looks down from heaven on the sons of men to see whether any understand and seek God* (Ps 13[14]:2); [28]and if every day the angels assigned to us report our deeds to the Lord day and night, [29]then, brothers, we must be vigilant every hour, or, as the Prophet says in the psalm, God may observe us *falling* at some time into evil and *so made worthless* (Ps 13[14]:3). [30]After sparing us for a while because he is a loving father who waits for us to improve, he may tell us later, *This you did, and I said nothing* (Ps 49[50]:21).

• • •

This long first step divides the human person into these constitutive elements: mind (source of thoughts), will (source of personal direction) and body (instrument of interaction but, alas, frequently, the slave of appetites). It relates the human person, so conceived, to God who is supreme and the worthy object of our fear and vigilance. St. Benedict speaks, in good biblical tradition, of a healthy fear of God, one that accords God his honor and the majesty due his name, without the servile fear that cripples the heart and stunts the theological mind. But healthy fear is a rarity at any time. All too often, our image of God is taken from the faulty authority models which have been foisted on us as innocent children. Before the spiritual director or novice director attempts to explicate the Rule any further than this point, one must explore the image of God at work in the disciple.

Step 1, vv. 10-11: Trying to live the Rule with a merciless or abusive God breathing over one's shoulder is a recipe for sure disaster. It quickly surfaces. Obsessive-compulsive traits emerge as the person desperately tries to keep God from correcting, or flying off into a violent tirade or worse. Because there is little comfort gleaned from the normal sources, such as prayer or *lectio divina,* and because relaxation in the solitude of woods or fields cannot rid one of a faulty image of God, afflicted persons end up by carrying a cage around for their own imprisonment. There is little self confidence but a lot of self doubt. In order to shield oneself as best as possible, one hides behind observances rigidly followed in hopes that this will appease the thunderous God inside the head. And as one spends more and more time trying to satisfy this insatiable God within, one withdraws more and more from the community of faith.

A person like this assumes that everyone else is caught in the same cage, and when others seem not to bother about their imprisonment, or when they seem not to care about this or that observance, in short, when they seem to our rigid monk to be slobs, fools or dolts, then the unfortunate monk adds insulting behavior to his other considerable problems. Anger and rage quickly fill the heart. Such a one is hard on others, and so the others quickly learn to avoid their stern and accusatory brother. In the end, the Rule becomes a slave driver and reinforces in the troubled brother an image of God precisely the opposite of the one it was written to foster.

When one has these tendencies, one should stay out of the monastery, or avoid monastic spirituality until sufficient theological maturity is achieved which can only be based on the experience of a loving God who calls one into the desert. The wet and fertile world outside is home for most people by God's very design. Here they can grow and develop according to the gentle plan of God's goodness. But the desert is a restricting climate where only the most adaptable species may grow. God intends such restriction only for those he has prepared for it. In fact, the desert tries to confound the natural way of growth so as to force a sublime evolution on the persons who struggle to live there. The desert is God's way of producing more quickly the ecstatic love of God which all people desire, but for which few are prepared to give their lives. In the desert, God can gift a person with the gospel desire for the heavenly kingdom even in the here and now. But such a person needs to know at the outset the risks involved and how difficult the task one has undertaken. When the saving will of God comes so close, it withers away all green growth and leaves only the bare stalk to survive.

Step 1, v. 11: A call to the desert, however, also includes a new kind of knowledge of God, one that is surely based on love, but a love which brooks no refusal. For there are only two ways in life. One leads to God, the other leads to destruction and hell. There is no third way. There is no neutral stance which opts out of the journey. This is the constant teaching in Revelation. "Happy are those who do not follow the advice of the wicked, nor take the path that sinners tread . . ."(Ps 1). The Rule encourages the neophyte to hurry along the way, to prefer nothing whatever to the love of Christ, to hasten with the footsteps of an eager heart. To refuse to do so after one has been called is to open oneself to the hopeless futility of having spurned God's love. True, we are sovereignly free to choose for or against God. But in choosing against God, we bring down on ourselves the worst kind of destruction.

Step 1, vv. 12-13: Vigilance over all behavior is recommended to the novice but under the law of obedience, silence and humility. These are easy enough to understand in the mind, and one may wholeheartedly agree with them in principle. But they begin to enter the heart when the first howls of loneliness and emptiness are heard from a harried novice. For the Rule allows companionship, food, diversion in work, etc., only at fixed times. Hands that reach out for support and camaraderie get slapped back. Hunger comes hard to one who is used to eating immediately when hungry. The Rule stands firm. The novice, like a pricked snail gone back to its shell, must learn to feed in solitude on deeper springs discovered in the Scriptures and monastic tradition if bitterness is not to drive one from monastic spirituality. What can one do but close the door on the screams, praying that some better life will awaken? No easy mitigations can be allowed to blunt the starkness of the landscape. Otherwise, it would not be the desert.

One can get pretty desperate trying to live the Rule. A kind of degrading temptation creeps into the thirsty mind: "Let me put out a possessive hand and make this my own. Let me savor an object, a person, a habit—something that is my very own, in which I am mirrored, which I can love as I used to." The flapping heart is forced to hear the dreaded words:

> ". . . without an order from the abbot, no one may presume to give, receive or retain anything as his own, nothing at all—not a book, writing tablets or stylus—in short, **not a single item**, especially since monks may not have the free disposal even of their own bodies and wills. For their needs, they are to look to the father of the monastery, and are not allowed anything which the abbot has not given or permitted" (RB 33.2-5).

Even the rich loam of talent desiccates in the desert. An identity nurtured in art must learn, often through inactivity or lack of a following, another kind of art—that of a faithful heart. If the art that one has developed is also part of Christ's call, then it must continue to be exercised in the monastery. A good rule of thumb is that, during the opening years of monastic living, the pursuit of one's art is controlled by a strict discipline set up in mutual agreement by the superiors and the artist. This ensures that the gift in question will be integrated into one's own monastic life and into the community in which one lives. If the community is never the recipient of one's talent, then the integration is suspect. On the other hand, one can use the community as a captive audience for second-rate stuff. Both extremes need to be avoided, but some evidence of both is inevitable. A long discernment must decide in the end whether or not a gift brought to the monastery can be developed with spiritual profit. St. Benedict provides the criterion in chapter 57 of the Rule:

"If one of them [the artisans] becomes puffed up by his skill-fulness in his craft, and feels that he is conferring something on the monastery, he is to be removed from practicing his craft and not allowed to resume it unless, after manifesting his humility, he is so ordered by the abbot" (RB 57.2-3).

These several considerations from the Rule spell out the kind of challenges the Rule poses and what kind of vigilance the monastic must adopt. Sins and vices of thought or tongue, of hand or foot take on new meaning when most of the common supports people take for granted are removed. For we enter the monastery with no preschooling, no preferment, no sponsor or tenure. As raw recruits, we take a place at the end of the line. We should take full advantage of being the last—at the tip of the tail, for we have only a brief time to appreciate the view it affords of the animal. Soon after, others will take their place at the end and will start us on our journey up through the body of the community in a kind of surge at once pleasing and painful. No logic attends this route, because rank is determined by the abbot and by the date, even the hour, of one's entry into the monastery. A junior may be someone in advance of the age of his senior. While the Rule allows for the natural feelings to go out to an elderly person, or to one who is very young, nevertheless, the time of conversion is the pattern of structure in the community. Fixing rank according to the time of conversion is a structure which bends the heart to the will of the Lord. Stripped of all expectation acquired previously, the monk now has only the grace of conversion with which to adorn his personality in this new society. One must guard that grace jealously, because that is all one has. Gratefully, the new-comer notes among the juniors the absence of struggle, ambition and dominance, where all that one has is given.

Step 1, vv. 14-18: The nun who endures several years of these opening trials may notice considerable growth. But one area which will continually trouble her will be her thoughts of comparison, envy or jealousy against her sisters. She can struggle against them as they surface, but, at the moment, there is little she can do to overcome them by reason or will power. For they are impervious to these; they are out of reach of the rational faculties. The best she can do is to note them and take them to God in prayer. What is wanted at this stage, and which is often not immediately forthcoming, is a new integration of heart, mind and will. In the beginning the mind debates with the gospel and is eventually defeated, if the grace of Christ is at work. The will may decide this or that, but the heart remains stunned and afraid. It will not connect in the ways it was made to. Only time lived by the Rule will gradually enable the heart to conduct itself according to the virtues which spring up spontaneously in wholesome thoughts. In the meantime, she must endure the ugliness of her own thoughts, but she must realize that, in turning to Christ, the ugliness has no power over her.

Newcomers cannot help but notice how others seem to receive more attention from the sisters than they do. Almost always, the abbess seems to affirm another more than herself. Massive powers of projection onto the community enable the nun to avoid the inner work and the inner pain that she is called to do and to suffer. It is not long before the zealous novice goes to the abbess or novice director with complaints about a double standard in the monastery. The elders seem not to have to live the Rule the way the novices are expected to live it. And how can the novices live the harshness of the Rule unless they are encouraged by the faultless example of the resident community? Frequently, eating becomes a source of scandal to those who think that abstemious habits at table come automatically with time spent in the monastery. Older members may enjoy eating more of a certain favorite dish. Newcomers notice the heaping helpings on other plates and think gluttony. But when their own favorite dish is served, and there is just enough for everyone to enjoy a little, and not enough to be sated, grumbling is likely to begin and rage in the heart unchecked for a while. The Rule foresees this case and others like it when it legislates for the amount of food in the refectory:

> "However, where local circumstances dictate an amount much less than what is stipulated above, or even none at all, those

who live there should bless God and not grumble. Above all else we admonish them to refrain from grumbling" (RB 40.8).

The awareness that one is murmuring does not come easily. For when I murmur against someone or something in the monastery, I would not do it unless I felt that I was justified. But self-justification is one of the steepest barriers to overcome at the beginning of the monastic journey. If, however, I keep my mind on the desert and its stark simplicity, I can sustain a sweetness of thought and be satisfied with almost anything that comes my way in the refectory or elsewhere.

Step 1, vv. 19-22: The Rule is uncompromising on the negation of the will and its desires. The novice feels, however, that he has kept his will pretty well in check simply by coming to the monastery. At the beginning and for some years, the novice will be convinced of the offering of his will to God. He looks back on the sudden change in direction his life took when he entered the monastery. Though he lived a moderately upright life, he marvels now at the depth of the renunciation to which he has been called. He remembers the confusion of the first days, the new feel in the body as early morning biorhythms made their first ungainly steps into territory long untrodden. First victories over pride come before his mind, and the first tears of loneliness. All that terrain has already been traversed. He feels secure in it. He takes his rest in it. Sometimes, he considers that the monastery is his savior, and that he has come here in reparation for a life wasted by sin. He may feel that the doors of opportunity had long since shut on a career full of defeat due to addiction, or the knowledge of sin, or the despair over the human condition. For him, monastic life is salvation, sweet and simple. If now his life is to bloom once again in the desert, that is all the more cause for rejoicing. For the penitent, the emphasis is on the isthmus of conversion, where, were it not for that grace, life would have been choked out. Whatever the case, the offering of the will in the first step of humility seems to have already been accomplished in most monastics. This is the first great cycle of offering. There are many more to follow.

Step 1, vv. 23-25: For the person of good zeal, the base desires of the body are held at bay for the opening years of the monastic life. The discipline introduced into the heart assumes an authority that one begins to trust and to rely on. That trust, in fact, is built up on the new energy that the person has on hand without asking or working for it in any obvious way. The life itself supplies more than one needs and allows a generosity at most of the observances. The rest seems strangely productive, and the monastic begins to love it, if ever so cautiously. To be sure, acedia is never far around the corner, lurking in wait for the unsuspecting soul. Yet, for most of the schedule as the seasons wind their way around the year, the monastic horarium takes good care of the body and provides it with a rhythm that is conducive to health and spiritual growth. One manifest wonder is that the monastic is able to spend enjoyable time with other members of the community which, had there been a choice, would not have been chosen companions before entering the monastery. If one were to take a closer look, however, one could see that potential problems loom on the horizon. Every few days, due to the rigors of the schedule or, what is more ominous, to a confrontational situation that is emotionally upsetting, compensatory overeating stuns the body. The unexpected offering of an irresistible snack ruins a fast. Sometimes, a day of sleep seems in order because one cannot endure another bout with drowsiness at meditation. You think, why fight this incessant losing battle? Why not adjust the schedule to fit my obvious physical needs? This may be the better part of prudence. But it just might as easily be the detour into a long-lost road where one wanders for months at a time. There is nothing serious here—only the warnings of battles ahead. Of sex, we make no mention, since the merciful God holds back this struggle until due time. In whatever the area, the battleground will be the body, and all the other components of the person seem to withdraw to let the battle be joined.

Step 1, vv. 26-30: With the number of breakthroughs and conversions occurring in her life, the nun now enjoys an image of God which no longer threatens or confronts her. She doesn't mind the eyes of the Lord on her at all times. She is becoming accustomed to it in the best possible sense. She expects it, and looks forward to it, and, in return, she offers her own vigilance over her heart as a sign of her fidelity. When the nun exercises a willing vigilance over the heart, she, in effect, is discovering her own heart knowledge. By this, we mean the knowledge that goes beyond feelings of good and ill, and beyond contentment and frustration. In abundance and in want, the nun knows that her heart is still in love and that it has been claimed by the Other. Though she is tempted to feel guilty over a fall, though her mood should swing to the right or to the left with a wide arc, she falls quickly to prayer. She knows that no matter what happens, God will draw her to prayer quite soon. This trust gives her an insouciance that is not arrogance, but the fruit of the first continual prayer. She becomes used to the idea of her own sin and infidelity, and so is not thrown by a momentary lapse, but rises immediately and goes on with her prayer, confident that contrition will re-emerge and restore her confidence in the tender mercy of God.

At some unknown point, the nun begins to realize that instead of her continual prayer to God in a steady vigilance, God's eyes are on her, not in judgment or in question, but in love. God takes the time to gaze on her continuously. Is this arrogance, or silliness to perceive God in this way? Or is it a growing awareness that contemplation is not something that she does but that God does by enlarging the ground of her being so that there is more of her for God to love and to act upon? In this way, the human person is made to be more like God because God makes the human person greater. Her vigilance becomes the route of approach by which God comes to her in care, consolation, and, above all, in his divine gaze of love. *Let the nun recall that she is always seen by God in heaven* . . . turns from a warning into a love song.

Our vigilance at every hour gives us a place in the spiritual world by insinuating our heart in God's love. That **place** has an *ordo* of its own internal organization. It begins as a desert, but is slowly transformed into an oasis of plenty and, ultimately, into a garden. It is nothing less than a garden of Christ's own remaking. He transforms the Garden of Adam and Eve into the garden where his own cross was planted and where he rose from the dead to complete his saving work in our midst.

Step Two: RB 7.31-33

[31]The second step of humility is that a man loves not his own will nor takes pleasure in the satisfaction of his desires; [32]rather he shall imitate by his actions that saying of the Lord: *I have come not to do my own will, but the will of him who sent me* (John 6:38). [33]Similarly we read, *Consent merits punishment; constraint wins a crown.*

• • •

The Search For The Will

The novice learns to associate first movements of grace with certain ascetical practices. Delighting in what seems to be a cause and effect relationship, she then goes about applying pressure to the human mechanism in order to achieve the desired control she has learned to enjoy. Commandments begin to be relished. Virtue and good habit start to build their own structures. Much of this activity is all too human. Certain telltale signs indicate a false truce in the struggle with evil. Whole sections of the personality are denied or ignored. Foremost in this denial is the refusal to search for the will which lies hidden beneath an ill-formed conscience. Some people go through their entire lives, even their religious lives, having gotten no further than the mere adoption of certain habits of behavior which ensure their place in the community. The old nun who clung to a thin spirituality through the turmoil of the Vatican Council years, but who never bothered, or was always afraid to let in new currents of thought, or more precisely, ancient truths of wisdom when they were made available to her, now finds herself isolated and bitter. Perhaps she clings to an unhealthy fasting with mixed motives of vanity and sanctity, and in the process has ruined her health. Such an elderly person is difficult to care for, because there is no getting past her fetish. Perhaps she has decided that the pre-council liturgy is the only true sacrament and will not hear of any liturgical reform. Whole communities have been ruined when the individual stance of a retired abbess, for instance, gets passed on to the entire community.

Younger persons can be helped more easily out of an ill-formed conscience, but sometimes the effort is risky. When the new monk comes to the community convinced that he has certain needs for his personal development and transfers this mind-set to his demands for the latest computer equipment, then he must learn to distinguish between legitimate needs and false needs which inhibit the necessary finding and offering of his own will. Many a pilgrim has left off the journey at this point.

Monastics of all ages should be on the lookout for the danger of turfdom. Having been given a job to do, they make it into their kingdom where no one else may enter. Everything is judged from the vantage point of staying protected inside their castle. A fundamental renunciation has not yet been made. Yet the mind can play tricks on them, convincing them that they have made all the proper negations to their own self-will, while blinding them to the fact that they stand in the midst of a burning fortress and the front gate is locked. They cannot get out, and no one else can get in to save them.

Jesus calls the person who is rich in commandments to follow further on towards the perfection of poverty, that is, the search for the will and the uncovering of its weakness. "Sell your possessions, and give the money to the poor, and you will have treasure in heaven; then come, follow me" (Matt 19:21). Unfortunately, many cannot leave the early wealth they have acquired; they spend years in the monastic life grieving over a spiritual blockage whose root causes they cannot uncover. For they have many moral possessions. They cling to their uprightness. Their memory of first penitence is shallow and short. They are still on spiritual milk and have not yet learned to trust the more solid food obtained by utter abandonment of one's own ephemeral goodness.

The Dialectic Of Weakness

The pain that often envelops a monastic in first vows, or even in the first years in solemn profession is the destruction of a sense of well-being brought on by the emergence of "issues." The attempt to fix a time in one's life when this phenomenon occurs is dangerous since many of us, in whatever walk of life we may be, continue to struggle with the pain of personal issues. Whether it be sexual misbehavior, codependency, career inadequacy, dysfunctional family of origin, or alcoholism, one or other of these issues works its way to the surface of consciousness and stirs up the waters of our day-to-day self. The silence and the solitude of the desert, plus the removal of the accustomed social supports and distractions allow these problems to emerge in ourselves, in our memory or in the lives of our loved ones. A thin-shelled persona, already battered by the blows of a competitive society, cracks apart under the rough treatment of monastic spirituality. If the monastic is thoroughgoing in discipline, the societal shield peals away all the faster. Easy self-assurance fades, and the hidden personality finds itself exposed to a probing and withering heat. A stalwart, healthy and vigorous personality, presumably, finds the wherewithal to deal with these first assaults on the conscience. Did they form the content of St. Paul's thorn in the flesh (see 2 Cor 12:7) or St. Anthony's earliest interior struggles?[3] Whether or not they did, these issues bring home to the monastic the reality of sin. "All have sinned and fall short of the glory of God" (Rom 3:23). Even when there is no moral wrongdoing along any of the issues mentioned above, a person must still deal with the sense of shame that constitutes our alienation from God. Along with the first emergence of a sense of sin, comes the deepened awareness of the boon of baptism. Whatever the conscience may awaken to, the heart that lives in grace trusts the salvation won for it by Jesus Christ and acknowledges the debt of love that is owed.

Whatever my particular share is in the burden of sin, it will fill my waking moments and lead me to a new sense of my moral weakness. Try as I might, I cannot seem to overcome my evil inclinations, the sweet but unlawful delight that infiltrates and putrefies my holiest moments. Where is my will, the will that brought me to the monastery, the will that fostered my

---

[3] Athanasius, *Vita Antonii*, PG 26, nos. 5–7, cols. 845–853. In English, *Athanasius*, "The Life of Antony," trans. and introd. Robert C. Gregg (New York: Paulist Press, 1980) nos. 5–7, pp. 33–37.

conversion, the will that turned my life around? Was it all God's actions on a paralyzed moral cripple? At some point in this self-examination, one asks the question: Can this be my responsibility, or is there some other force at work here, a force whereby I share in the collective guilt of humanity, just as Christ became sin for all of us, though he was sinless? Even if I sense that God has asked me to carry more than my own burden, there is no escaping my own guilt and failure. And if my spiritual drama is to have more than one act, then I must continue with that scene in Luke's Gospel where the penitent woman anoints the Lord's feet in the house of the Pharisee: "She stood behind him at his feet, weeping, and began to bathe his feet with her tears and to dry them with her hair. Then she continued kissing his feet and anointing them with the ointment" (Luke 7:38ff.).

When the Lord arises and straightens up the woman, and, according to St. Bernard, invites her to kiss him not only on the feet, but on the hands and on the mouth as well, then we may rest secure in a repentance that is rich in divine salvation. A mighty saga of love can be built on this foundation of sorrow, on which the personality is united and forged anew. What becomes habitual, and what runs through our drama, unifying and informing all, is not the refrain of the righteous, but the memory and misery of alienation from God overcome for us by Christ.

The search for God's forgiveness, coupled with a new self-knowledge, here called heart knowledge, is the first move toward the reconstruction of my dismantled self. As such, it is not really my move, but the initiative of Christ, as the author and finisher of our faith. God puts his finger, as it were, on the wounded will deep inside us. The very feeling of its pain as God touches it, reassures us that it was there all the time. It awakens to this transforming touch, and as it does so, it becomes the organ of trust in our penitent hearts. Very slow progress along the weakness that bothered us the most begins to be felt. The progress fires the flame of continuous prayer as the heart warms to its exercise. Still, the process is intermittent, not all the time. For we are as yet very weak. Other aspects of the revelation need to be learned in the heart and in the new-found will at this time.

When we reason with God why he chose to take us on so painful a journey, the answer comes in the form of Scripture. "But law came in, with the result that the trespass multiplied; but where sin increased, grace abounded all the more . . ." (Rom 5:20-21). As we find our own wounded will, we also find the grace of Christ in his saving mystery. We cling to Christ as our Savior, as the one who gently lowered us into this caldron of self-knowledge so that he might lift us up by his mercy. The greater the sin, the more powerful the grace to save, and the more particularly felt is the saving. "Therefore, I tell you, her sins, which were many, have been forgiven; hence she has shown great love. But the one to whom little is forgiven, loves little" (Luke 7:47).

Here another doctrine of Christology comes clear to the mind. The will of God in sending Christ was that "I [Christ] should lose nothing of all that he has given me, but raise it up on the last day" (John 6:39); and: "I give them eternal life, ... No one will snatch them out of my hand" (John 10:28). Also: "While I was with them, I protected them in your name that you have given me. I guarded them, and not one of them was lost except the one destined to be lost" (John 17:12).

Jesus continues that promise in the monastic life at the time of vows. For the abbot of the monastery is commanded by the Rule to

> ". . . so accommodate and adapt himself to each one's charac-
> ter and intelligence that he will not only keep the flock en-
> trusted to his care from dwindling, but will rejoice in the
> increase of a good flock. . . . The abbot must know that any-
> one undertaking the charge of souls must be ready to account
> for them" (RB 2.32, 37).

The goal in the formation of a monastic spirituality obviously revolves around the thirst and the seeking for God. If the
novice finds joy in the desert, and consents to be led by Christ
into the Garden of the Passion, there to undergo in her own
heart something of the weakness and alienation from God that
Christ suffered for all of us in Gethsemane, then she can rest in
the death brought on by the dialectic of weakness. Her own
moral strength and weakness are now united in his death and

resurrection. In him, her two are one. Little by little, her flesh, heart, mind and memory will begin to be redeemed because her will has been found, touched and united. A new person, called before the foundation of the world, will begin to emerge. The very life of God, shared through her faith, will begin to be her principle of living.

Step Three: RB 7.34

[34]The third step of humility is that a man submits to his superior in all obedience for the love of God, imitating the Lord of whom the Apostle says: *He became obedient even to death* (Phil 2:8).

•••

Religious obedience comes to be misunderstood as childish by people who see in it leftovers from medieval society still existing in ghettoes of superstitious religious communities. Because of the emphasis today on the sovereignty of the individual, our culture carries a handicap to the proper appreciation of obedience. In fact, an accurate sense of religious obedience does nothing but confirm our own best intuitions of autonomy and freedom, granted, of course, that one is able to accept the spirituality and the theology that stand behind it. And here is the difficulty.

Obedience never separates itself from humility before God because obedience re-establishes God's sovereignty over the world and especially over myself and my circle. This stance before God, by shattering my apparent self-validation, humbles me before God and also before my neighbor. But if I can accept this first principle, then my neighbor becomes not my adversary, or even my friend, but my brother and sister in God, whom I love as myself. The fundamental move then is from being self-centered to God-centered and, of course, other-oriented.

I consider myself not as a local autonomous noble, competing savagely with many such noble folk for my piece of the social pie. Instead, I acknowledge the human community and my place in it. Where it is appropriate, I sacrifice something of my own autonomy in order to belong to the group. In a properly

Christian perspective, I serve the group. I obey the others. I live no longer for myself but for God, who, in Christ, gave himself up for me and my neighbor.

I move from making a sacrifice of my own autonomy to co-operation with the others, to adherence to the community, and finally, to love of my community. This includes obedience to the authority to which we have all agreed. I understand the constant dialectic between responsibility for my own well-being before God, and obedience to whatever group to which I belong. My growth as a person cannot be distinguished from this tension.

Therefore, obedience plays a necessary part of everyone's life, at all times, and acts as the doorway for their deepest desires, unless they choose to live at war with everyone else who does not serve their needs.

In considering all these aspects, I am able to consider Christ and to imitate him who obeyed God even unto death, trusting that his center could not be fulfilled unless he gave it over to God and God's designs for him. By considering Christ in this way, I move spiritual considerations to theological ones. I trust in God's action in my own life, that God stands behind the communities to which I adhere, and their authorities. I believe that God directs my life according to his own will through them. A mature obedience presupposes a love and an understanding of how God works in human lives. This is why St. Bernard could speak so exultingly of the gift of obedience in monastic life.

He writes that one can obey authority out of a fear of reprisal, or because of one's conviction of principle. One can elevate the obedience by obeying another out of a love of God, thereby substituting charity for law. But obedience is perfect, according to St. Bernard, "when the command is received in the spirit in which it is given. When the will of the subject is conformed to that of the superior, the subject, in carrying out his orders, will not be likely to confuse greater matters with lesser or lesser with greater (as often happens)."[4]

---

[4] *Sancti Bernardi Opera* (Roma: Editiones Cistercienses, 1963) vol. III, *Tractatus et Opuscula*, "De Praecepto et Dispensatione," n. 16, lines 10–15.

I can conform my will to that of the abbot only when I am free enough to be master of my own will. As we have seen in the previous pages, this is no small matter. Monastic obedience worthy of the name, does not confuse childish conformity with loving cooperation in mature personhood. The greater the person I am, the more easily comes a sense of obedience, simply because it takes great self mastery, as a gift from God, to obey maturely. This kind of obedience is in direct imitation of Christ, as the Rule suggests. Obedience on such an exalted level should not be discussed too lightly by those who do not believe in this kind of divine transformation, or in the greatness of the human person. This realm can only be entered by faith, where faith is a share in the life of God.

When this kind of obedience comes to life in the human heart, then we have passed from the desert of monastic life, through the Garden of Adam and Eve, into the Garden of Gethsemane, and onto the Garden where the Tree of Life grows. Though there is still much ground to cover, the person who has begun to be so remade, starts to enjoy the hundredfold reward which Jesus promised. Things that were renounced for the sake of the kingdom, are rediscovered in the new creation. That new world has already begun to be revealed in one whose heart has been resurrected with Christ. The beginnings of the new creation rest on the foundation of faith, which nothing now can shake, because it is built on the rock of Christ, who has come to dwell in the heart in the full strength of his resurrection.

A word of caution is in order concerning the desert, the garden, and their fulfillment. We are not speaking here of definitive states, but of a process of ever-increasing faith, hope and love. We must accustom ourselves to a revolving door which spins us now into the desert, the garden or the fulfillment. As we travel with the revolving door, each of these three becomes more real, more luminous. We come to understand how the desert is really the garden, and the garden is really the

---

In English, *The Works of Bernard of Clairvaux* vol. 1, Treatises I, Cistercian Fathers Series, no. 1 (Spencer, Mass: Cistercian Publications, 1970) "On Precept and Dispensation," no. 16, p. 116.

fulfillment, depending on the depth of our understanding and the strength of our faith. Those who are advanced take them on with insouciance, delighting to be filled, but not minding the lean times. For the constant vigil has allowed them to become indifferent, and their spiritual eye has perfected its skills.

Novices naturally grow impatient with this process, or, I should say, the long, slow acquiring of spiritual sensibility. The monastic tradition speaks curtly about neophyte strategy: "If thou seest a young man ascending up to heaven by his own will, catch him by the foot and throw him down, for it is not expedient for him."[5]

The first raw energies released by the Desert-Garden experience suggest opportunity which if not grasped, is lost forever. The bright and the anxious think to seize it and to advance themselves. But the gradual elevation of humility, a long barely rising trail, is the only way of ascent for the proud-minded. The suggestion that sudden enlightenment has been bestowed, because they always suspected that they were great (when, strangely, no one else did), is a deadly trap for talented newcomers. Convinced that holiness lies behind an inviolate wall of perfect observance and a rigid schedule, they bend only when broken by ill health of body or mind. Some break out of discretion like a hernia, and push silence or some other ascetic practice to the point of being obnoxious to the brethren, or so distant that they are not in the same community with them. Still others cannot accept their bodily weakness and so make indulgent adjustments to a schedule they then follow rigidly. But for the spiritually astute, sickness, weakness, and even a certain sloppiness present special opportunities. For God means us to use even this towards our enlightenment. Evagrius gives wise advice on true progress:

> One is not always in a position to follow his usual rule of life but one must always be on the alert to seize the opportunities to fulfill all the duties possible to the best of his powers. The demons are not ignorant of the possibilities offered them on

[5] *Vitae Patrum* V, PL 73, trans. Pelagius, *Verba Seniorum* X, n. 111. English trans., Helen Waddell, *The Desert Fathers* (Ann Arbor, Mich.: University of Michigan Press, 1957) 16.

such occasions. Thus it happens that in their passion against us they prevent our fulfilling what is possible and constrain the sick from giving thanks while undergoing pain and from bearing patiently with the various ministrations they require. Again they encourage the weak to feats of fasting and those who are weighed down with illness of standing on their feet for prolonged periods.[6]

High-spirited persons will probably suffer many years of excess, discouragement and backsliding before they get the balance right. When they finally begin to accept tranquility, they will look back and see how their own demons made them look like fools. But they will not care for long. Having arrived at faith and that strength of soul which gives true peace, they will have compassion on themselves, and laugh gently and appreciatively at their years of labor.

---

[6] Evagrius Ponticus, *Praktikos (Traité Pratique ou Le Moine)*, eds. Antoine and Claire Guillaumont, Sources chrétiennes 171 (Paris: Editions du Cerf, 1971) ch. 40, pp. 592–593. In English, *Praktikos and Chapters on Prayer*, trans. John Eudes Bamberger, Cistercian Studies 4 (Spencer, Mass.: Cistercian Publications, 1970) ch. 40, p. 27.

CHAPTER FIVE

The Promised Land:
The Steps of Humility 4–8

In God's plan, the people of Israel are always moving forward to the Promised Land. Even when their camp is not on the move, but is pitched somewhere in the wilderness, their imagination is pinned to the promise of the land flowing with milk and honey. The promise is a retaining wall which supports their present life. Without it, their life in the here and now would be scattered into fragments without meaning.

In the opposite direction from the promised land stand the Red Sea and the Egypt which was left behind. The conversion from Egypt contributes as much to the present as the promise. When the people were gathered by Moses to rise up and break with their slavery, they experienced God's saving deed at the Red Sea as a people—a redeemed community. They accepted an embryonic covenant of obedience with the God who heard their cry for help. No longer would they calculate the future for themselves, but they would move, act and pray as the people of God. Two fundamental boundaries form the people of Israel—their conversion from Egypt, and their move towards the Promised Land.

In the same way, the monastic moves out from another kind of Egypt—the negativity and chaos at loose in our contemporary culture—and, crossing the Red Sea at the entrance to the monastery, sojourns with the community in the desert of monastic life. The newcomer to monastic life does not leave the world so much as chooses only certain things from it in order to create a world within a world. In so doing, the monastic seeks a world blessed by prudent choices made in the light of the Holy Spirit. This holy place can become unholy if the monastic clings to it as if it were an end in itself. But if it grows to be a means to the making of a more spiritual community, then the monastery can become a catalyst for good far beyond its walls. The monastic person can bring down and spread abroad the mercy of God for all others. From space and time, the monastic seeks to introduce the reality of eternity into a specific and historical place, be it the monastic community or the person himself. Just as with the people of Israel, the conversion to eternity which was begun in the past, and the look towards the future, are the two most important elements of the monastic's life. Without them, monastic life would only be a caricature of itself and another cultural phenomenon on a sterile landscape of sameness.

Let us recall for a moment the way in which God implants us in the land to which he has called us, for it will provide the key to unlock the mystery of our further move into the Promised Land. The misery and discipline of the first years of monastic living must not be lessened or mitigated by a well meaning superior or guide. For God uses them as a tool to dig in the human heart and plant his eternal Word. The first images of and associations with the land shine on the heart like light on unexposed film. "I lift up my eyes to the hills—from where will my help come?" (Ps 121:1). Mountains and meadows that have witnessed the bare chest heaving with loneliness and nostalgia, become companions on the journey, become supporting aunts and uncles, bosom friends, partners by bonding. Special glades, small lakes, diminutive valleys of the monastery property take on the scale of whole regions where our orbit has room to turn and breathe fresh to the sun. Our story is branded on the land. And the pain is softened by tears. Long after, these places of bonding will hold on to the human spirit as it longs to be free of the tension of the monastery which God has allowed to increase. For the humility which we learned in the first three steps of our journey must now be tested under fire and heat by the steps of the second stage. The faith that was laid as a foundation in the very soil of the land must now support a superstructure of hope which is high up, open to the air, and catching the breeze of distant lands. The second stage is when God asks a greater sacrifice. But God could not ask it if the first stage had not been claimed.

The Journey of the Word

The Scriptures, and especially the psalms of the Liturgy of the Hours become the land into which we sink our roots. They soak up every emotion the nun has to vent, serenely, impassively. Aesthetical musing, drooping fatigue, rapacious hunger, anger—all are received by the liturgy with uncalloused hands. Pockets full, arms ready to ministry, the liturgy waits for the unusual moment when the nun's spirit is tame, to let fall on her tongue a drop of the praise of God, and a richer savor of the paschal mystery, Christ's own Red Sea experience. Then, she is swallowed up again by the rough and tumble of her thoughts. The liturgy turns the color she does, matching wave for wave of whatever emotion holds the sway at that moment. Churned up seabed from the past requires time and many calm days to dissipate itself. This, too, the liturgy will provide, for it remains stronger than any personal turbulence. Endless in its suffering and patience, it waits to reveal to its children that which it longs to make manifest—the love of God in Christ, the face of Christ in all his manifold wisdom, in every human emotion now treated and transformed and made beautiful. The nun begins to trust every feeling to this parent. Fidelity, chaste love and tender respect begin to shape the nun's response to the liturgy. Black clouds of spite and ugliness, or the fog of boredom and distaste may linger on for many years, but the dominant response eventually cleanses itself into the joy of pure praise. The fusion of life and liturgy may now take place in the nun in a definitive way. The promise of transformation in Christ can now start to be fulfilled. Often, the nun does not even reflect anymore on the memory of her first insight in the Psalms. For the memory continually grows with new insight. It never has time to grow old, or to be detached from its source in actuality, or to become a memory in the usual sense. The only glimpse of it the nun may get is when she is away from the monastery and the choir. The absence of the habit of the liturgy and its cleansing effect will soon be felt. Despite the strangeness of the separation, it has its value. For, when back home, she will cling to the liturgy all the more. And she may begin to define herself as a living memory of Christ, that is, one who is always remembering Christ in the Psalms.

God, in his Word, is not only the ground where we are anchored, but also the movement of our destiny. As the second stage of "proceeding" begins, the Word becomes the pillar of cloud to lead us to another place even as we traverse the land which is already God. Paradoxically, the journey of the Word is into the vast ground of the heart. If mind, heart and will are ready, then the practice of *lectio divina* will become our place of battle with the demons of the past. The Word will strengthen us for this assault because it will journey with us into our own psyche, to find those places which feed our negative thoughts and feelings. God is willing to do the spade work there, drilling into the veins of imagination, into the crevices of the heart's desires, tapping into the rivulets of attraction and repulsion, all of which make up our personality. During this extended journey of autobiography, rewritten now in the light of God's Word, notebooks and journals, psychologists and analysts are usually in order. The process of self-knowledge as a way of life is embraced. A time of nurturing becomes normative. This self-scrutiny need take only so long as God wills. Yet it seems for monastics that God has long years in mind, the proverbial forty years of wandering to find the Promised Land within.

The journey down into the land represents a more stable period where the emphasis is off newness and on adaptation and steady monotonous work. The abbot and the leaders of the community, as well as one's closest associates take on a more obvious role. They point out for us, and sometimes they are, the land flowing with milk and honey. But like the spies whom Moses sent out to reconnoiter the land, they must also warn us sojourners of the fierce foes which must be driven out before the promised land can be occupied successfully. Stability on our own land is never just easy squatting. For each piece of tranquility claimed, we must confront and control some wild energy within, or some bullying foe without. At times great decisive victories may be won; but for the most part, we take a few steps forward, and then a few backward, against an enemy which never seems to be fully subdued. Although one must be cautious, looking this way and that, one may finally begin to plow and prepare the land; small fields of crops are planted and a modest harvest is taken in. Only in hindsight can we see through the routine to the significant events of confrontation, growth, and self-knowledge which are the actual planting and harvesting. For the moment, it all seems so regular and unimportant. Nevertheless, time spent on the land is what makes it historical, "freighted with social meanings derived from historical experience."[1]

Gradually, over a period of time, the monk may start to apply to himself the saying of Our Lord: "Other seeds fell on good soil and brought forth grain, some a hundredfold, some sixty, some thirty" (Matt 13:8).

Noticing that obedience comes a little easier, or that restraint of speech has become slightly more natural, the monk feels the growing strength of virtue in the heart. He begins to apply to himself what he thinks caused the growth—the appropriation of monastic teaching he has heard in conferences or read in *lectio divina*. Encouraged, he reads on, listens more attentively, and applies more vigorously what he has learned and understood. Step by step, his life takes on purpose. The beginnings of a goal take shape in the mind. Here the abbot or the spiritual director needs to be ready at hand to suggest images and ways of thinking about the growth experiences which the monk shares with him. When purpose gradually orders the monk's life, so that he can articulate it, then the abbot may want to suggest *puritas cordis* to the novice, or *tranquilitas*, or some other monastic ideal. The timing needs to be right, and the suggestions delicate. The plant might just thrive. Depending on the sensitivity of the monk, he may discern an

---

[1] Walter Brueggemann, *The Land: Place as Gift, Promise, and Challenge in Biblical Faith* (Philadelphia: Fortress, 1977) 2.

overall order to his experiences of growth. If so, he will probably apply more purpose, in order to bring about the desired effect. So, **growth, purpose and order** constitute the first great cycle of stability on the land. The growth is unwieldy, ungainly, and crashes occur. But new energy has been released throughout the person; and this energy, once tasted, pushes the monk's roots deeper into the soil. It is at this point that the dreaded fourth and fifth steps of humility occur.

Step Four: RB 7.35-43

[35]The fourth step of humility is that in this obedience under difficult, unfavorable, or even unjust conditions, his heart quietly embraces suffering [36]and endures it without weakening or seeking escape. For Scripture has it: *Anyone who perseveres to the end will be saved* (Matt 10:22), [37]and again, *Hope in him, hold firm and take heart. Hope in the Lord!* (Ps 26[27]:14). [38]Another passage shows how the faithful must endure everything, even contradiction, for the Lord's sake, saying in the person of those who suffer, *For your sake we are put to death continually; we are regarded as sheep marked for slaughter* (Rom 8:36; Ps 43[44]:22). [39]They are so confident in their expectation of reward from God that they continue joyfully and say, *But in all this we overcome because of him who so greatly loved us* (Rom 8:37). [40]Elsewhere Scripture says: *For you, O God, have tested us, you have tried us as silver is tried; you led us, God, into the snare; you laid a heavy burden on our backs* (Ps 65[66]:10-11). [41]Then, to show that we ought to be under a superior, it adds: *You have placed men over our heads* (Ps 65[66]:12).

[42]In truth, those who are patient amid hardships and unjust treatment are fulfilling the Lord's command: *When struck on one cheek, they turn the other; when deprived of their coat, they offer their cloak also; when pressed into service for one mile, they go two* (Matt 5:39-41). [43]With the Apostle Paul, they bear with *false brothers, endure persecution,* and *bless those who curse them* (2 Cor 11:26; 1 Cor 4:12).

•••

The difficult, unfavorable or even unjust conditions mean adversarial situations. They could be of three different kinds. The "difficult" conditions could be the reappearance of personal issues in the nun's heart. She struggles against them, but she seems to be unable to dislodge them from their position inside her. Suppose the abbess asks her to do a work that brings these issues to the fore, say, to manage a work area when she feels herself to be ineffective at motivating people. She knows that the abbess has this very difficulty of hers in mind, and that the abbess is asking her to do this disagreeable work precisely to occasion growth. She doubts her own ability and the wisdom of the abbess. Can she detect some hidden malice in the abbess's request?

"Unfavorable" conditions frequently have to do with personality clashes at the work place. Persons who are jealous of us, or who raise up unsuspected envy in us, inevitably appear in our lives at the daily job. Who sets up these nagging and bothersome proximities? Why, by a single appointment or direction, would a boss or a superior or an employer choose to cloud over our sun with endless dreary weather?

Of "unjust" treatment, much could be said, but little should be said if we are going to avoid delving into nasty business. For here we are speaking of sick persons loose in a community or family or church or workplace. Where no one has seen fit in the past to curb or remove a disturbed person, the present regime contents itself to conceal the troublesome one within the bosom of an institution, convinced, perhaps a little too conveniently, that this is the charitable thing to do. Perhaps the sick person has rights that the authority fears to abrogate. By not addressing the lesser evil in the individual, a greater evil has been allowed to grow and adversely affect a whole family or community. Clearly, the rights of one person are not absolutes in themselves, but must be weighed against the good and the rights of others. There is always the possibility, too, that the authority has simply misjudged the situation, and in so doing, grants the sick person the authority to determine just what rights he or she has over against the community. Once established, these ill-gotten rights become the fiercely protected possessions of the sick one. Troubled persons have an uncanny ability for self-defense. They can manage to turn any therapeutic move against their illness into an unjust attack by malicious people. Only strong and clear vision on the part of the authority can resist this trickery on the part of the diseased. Unfortunately, while the community or family or institution suffers collectively, a lone individual or individuals take(s) the brunt of the violence dished out by the sick one. And here is where the fourth step accurately portrays the internal struggle of one who is carrying the burden of righteousness for the group.

In order to help the heart to "quietly embrace suffering and endure it without weakening or seeking escape," the Rule provides certain passages from Scripture, which, when internalized, offer a structure of endurance as well as discernment. "Wait for the Lord; be strong and let your heart take courage; wait for the Lord!" (Ps 26[27]:14). This psalm passage directs the sufferer beyond the litter of wreckage in his own person to the Lord alone. It presupposes a faith strong enough to bypass all the threats to one's own personhood and well being the negative assaults can hurl. It allows one's defenses to stay low when they want to be raised. A relatively innocent and healthy person walks around with little or no armor. She is not expecting or looking for trouble. When attacked, she is not quick to defend herself. Instead, self doubt based on self knowledge quickly rallies to form a judgment that the thrust of an adversary was justified. She must discern quickly that either she is not the problem, or that she shares in part of the problem but not the whole of it. Then she can take the suffering beyond herself, further than her guilt, and posit it where it ultimately belongs, at the Cross of Christ. For only at the Cross, can the hope which Truth offers be fulfilled.

"No, in all these things we are more than conquerors through him who loved us" (Rom 8:37). We do not carry our Cross alone. There is one who has gone before us, who came to meet us with the blessings of his own victory. Where everything else has been lost, when treachery seems to be leering at us to weaken our faith, we have only to consider the love of him by whom we were saved. This love is stronger than our death, mightier even than hell. Though we may go to a kind of death in order to reach it, this love grants us a kind of energy to seek this love to the end, regardless of the price to ourselves. In this we transcend ourselves and know that a power, at once old and new, has overtaken us and given us rest.

"For you O God, have tested us . . ."(Ps 65[66]:10-11). The very authority which once gave growth and structure to our lives, is now the dreaded voice of discipline and self-sacrifice. The abbot who received us and nurtured us, the institution that sponsored us, the spouse that loved us, these are the very persons who, in the middle years, seem to turn on a lover or a subordinate with demands which to us seem outrageous. All that was once built up, they now seem to be pulling down. And we are left powerless, because we hesitate to turn on the hand which once fed us. We look to God who seems to have led us into this snare. He has placed this affliction on our backs.

We reflect that in trying to be faithful to the God who called us into the community, into an institution, into a marriage, we have been duped as was Jeremiah. We feel betrayed by God. The irrationality of the situation gets compounded by the fact that we see that the purpose which attended our growth has been reversed. Senseless and useless seems the suffering, and what's more, destructive. Yet, out of love for God whom we cannot deny, we allow that our suffering is for God's sake. And in this thought, we find meaning. "For your sake we are being killed all day long; we are accounted as sheep to be slaughtered" (Rom 8:36).

The order that we had made out of our desert has been torn apart. The garden that we worked has been plowed under. The injustice we now experience assumes the quality of persecution. Far from being vague and obscure, the negativity is proactive, determined and focused by its anger, or so it seems. What we once thought applied to Jesus alone in the perfect injustice of the Cross, now appears to have landed on our front door. This realization changes forever how we meditate on the passion of Jesus. For that persecution is now our own. The absolutely impossible preaching of the Sermon on the Mount has come down to our own lowly person. "But if anyone strikes you on the right cheek, turn the other also; and if anyone wants to sue you and take your coat, give your cloak as well; and if anyone forces you to go one mile, go also the second mile" (Matt 5:39-41). We never thought we were worthy of so exalted a word. Yet now it resides in our own shirt. With St. Paul we cry out, "Wretched man that I am! Who will save me from this body of death?" (Rom 7:24).

At this point in our difficulty, we need to take a step back and get a different perspective. Growth, purpose and order, even if blessed by God and raised up by him in the opening years of our monastic living, must always contend with darker powers and contrary forces. We cannot escape the human condition, nor the mysterious presence of evil at every turn. Jesus reminds us of this fact in the parable of the wheat and the weeds: "Let both of them [the wheat and the weeds] grow together until the harvest; and at harvest time I will tell the reapers, 'Collect the weeds first and bind them in bundles to be burned, but gather the wheat into my barn'" (Matt 13:30).

Jesus implies that evil will always be found mixed with the good before the judgment. We cannot escape this reality. Even within ourselves, our spiritual growth does not occur without the appearance of some parasite: ". . . but while everybody was asleep, an enemy came and sowed weeds among the wheat, and then went away. So when the plants came up and bore grain, then the weeds appeared as well" (Matt 13:25-26).

We are hard-pressed, too, to determine whether all the evil comes from outside ourselves. Our own growth in self-knowledge has already indicated to us how compromised we are in ourselves. We need always to keep this anguished truth before our eyes, even as we learn to discern the truth about the ugliness of our neighbor. In fact, the painful consideration of an objective injustice, where there can be no doubt as to the truth of it, also leads us to an increasing awareness of our own frailty and the ambiguous nature of our intentions.

To the person who has been faithful in a relationship, or in a community, the unjust attack of a neighbor or friend is fraught with consequences. Enmity in the monastic community puts extra strain on the quality of one's stability. For we have been told to keep close to the bosom of the group, never seeking our desires outside of the monastic fraternity. St. Benedict insisted that the monastery go to great lengths to insure that everything could be done within the monastic enclosure. What happens when at every corner our enemy seems to appear? All the familiar places in a household turn to poison when a marriage disintegrates. The dearest thing once shared becomes a torture and a taunt. Our whole space is polluted. The trenchant words of the fourth step on endurance must now be obeyed. The inner spoliation is indeed severe.

From endurance we pass to perseverance. The first reaction, upon realizing that a significant part of our world has turned against us, is to withdraw. People leave employments most frequently because of the inability or unwillingness to sustain their position in an adversarial atmosphere. Divorce is the usual escape route when marriage partners lose intimacy. In a monastic community, where the emotional field is more constant, but perhaps less intense than that of a household, there is a great temptation simply to withdraw emotionally. Merely to avoid the places where sister X goes, to ask the superior for a work assignment where brother Y will not be, to stay on this side of the room when so and so is on that side, is an effective but very costly way to avoid contact with the troublesome party. For a while this solution may be advisable. Ultimately, however, it is not good for us, and disastrous for them.

It is not good for us because it ruins our growth on the land, our stability. How else can a water shoot, bursting out of a branch of a tree, itself become a sturdy branch, if it insists on dying back at the first adverse attack of the weather? How does the earth turn vegetation into the ooze of oil beneath the surface without the staying power of centuries? How can anything produce something else if the connections are pulled away? If we pull away emotionally from our unpleasant situation, the program is over, the television goes dark, there is no more show. We must leave and begin again, working very hard to accomplish no more than we did the last time. A similar situation will form itself a second time, and the cycle will begin all over.

To cut the connections is even worse for the other party because we are removing the opportunity for confrontation and correction. We have let the worst part of them gain a victory which cements them in their illness. The good part of them, hidden deep below their violent surface behavior, will never be allowed to emerge as long as they can get what they want by unlawful means. Their pain is too great, their needs too overwhelming for them not to use the victory they have secured. But if they had no victory, if the alcoholic had no drink, if the violent could not crush the just one, if the egotist could not bully a way through the crowd, then they might be forced to consider other options, and, perhaps, even the truth. To withdraw from a sick one is to send them into exile as Cain was driven over the face of the earth with the mark of the murderer on his forehead.

Moving on towards salvation, even in adversity, lies at the base of the monastic teaching on stability. There are only two ways to move, either forward or backward. The way backward is the plausible way, wide and comforting and well traveled. The way forward is narrow and rough, even forbidding. It requires determination fueled by grace to set out on this way. But to stand still in the face of this dilemma is to hear the condemnation of the Lord: "No one who puts a hand to the plow and looks back is fit for the kingdom of God" (Luke 9:62). It would be better to run away than to be lukewarm, lingering around until a third or middle way becomes visible. There is no middle way. When the time of decision comes, just like the Bridegroom in the middle of the night, one must be ready to light one's lamp and go out at once to meet him. Otherwise the opportunity is lost and we are left with nothing and no one but ourselves and the other foolish ones who felt the same way.

Finally, to embrace the suffering, after having learned to endure it and to persevere in it, is to turn a negative situation into a positive one. The text of the Rule uses the words: "the heart quietly embraces suffering." This suggests a wholly different level of experience than the turmoil of the emotions. To the one who follows the teaching of stability, a deeper discovery is granted: the gift of tranquility, with all the passions calmed and the mind cleared and ready for action. For, beneath all of the whipped up waves, there lies deep on the ocean floor a peace that is the home only of those creatures that can sustain the weight and pressure of the water. Surprisingly, at that depth, the yoke is easy and the burden is light, precisely because we are not carrying it. The Lord of heaven and earth has already carried that burden, and is still carrying it for us. When we are willing to follow his call to the depths where all is won and all is at peace, then we hand over our difficulties to him and to his power to save.

Step Five: RB 7.44-48

⁴⁴The fifth step of humility is that a man does not conceal from his abbot any sinful thoughts entering his heart, or any wrongs committed in secret, but rather confesses them humbly. ⁴⁵Concerning this, Scripture exhorts us: *Make known your way to the Lord and hope in him* (Ps 36[37]:5). ⁴⁶And again, *Confess to the Lord, for he is good; his mercy is forever* (Ps 105[106]:1; Ps 117[118]:1). ⁴⁷So too the Prophet: *To you I have acknowledged my offense; my faults I have not concealed.* ⁴⁸*I have said: Against myself I will report my faults to the Lord, and you have forgiven the wickedness of my heart* (Ps 31[32]:5).

•••

At an earlier stage of the spiritual life, the fifth step aids the person to self disclose to the abbot or spiritual guide. But at a later stage, such as we have described in the commentary above for the fourth step, a different view point may be taken. Now the abbot must be ready to receive the confidence of a person who is attempting to carry the burden of unjust or unfair treatment. Can this guide understand the dilemma that is presented? Can this superior appreciate the discernment that is asked, namely, that of determining whether or not the person can bear the tension of unjust treatment fruitfully?

In the case of a monastic community, it is often the superior who is responsible for the crucible that the monk finds himself in. The perpetrator monk may be holding the abbot hostage in order to defend his own territory. The abbot is reluctant to move against him, and prefers to let the rest of the community deal with him in its own way. When this is the case, then individuals will get hurt and they will need to unburden themselves to a wise guide. Is the abbot the person to direct them? How many superiors consider how they might be ruining weaker individuals when they allow a sick person loose in the community? If the situation cannot be helped, then they certainly need to support with all tenderness the sufferings of those who are troubled unjustly in the community.

When a spiritual guide is presented with a situation of complex enmeshment and co-dependency, she must be wary of giving advice too soon. Only with careful discernment can she determine whether or not the person who is seeking advice can take the terrible words of stability, endurance and perseverance. Very few persons are prepared to receive the unadulterated teaching of the gospel. Still, it must be remembered that Jesus did not hesitate to give the disciples the teaching of the Sermon on the Mount.

The discernment which the abbess must make is whether or not the nun can suffer the ruin of one of her lives, with all the pain that accompanies closed doors and frustrations unto death, and like the butterfly, emerge from that cocoon with a new set of wings that enable her to fly off into eschatological hope. This is not mere metaphor. What happens to the nun in religious life? The discernment not to withdraw may mean that, with certain doors closed to her, even though she pined for the rooms of emotional comfort, the nun may be forced to enter the narrow door that makes her stronger. She may even grow into a wisdom figure, one who has suffered, endured and radiates peace. She may become a fertile tree where others can come for rest and shade. Is it any different for a partner in a failed marriage? To stay in such a marriage may mean many lost opportunities, even enormous sacrifice in order to remain faithful. What kind of a life is left to the healthy partner when shame, abuse or neglect are the daily diet? Few have the grace to endure such hardship. Still, the discernment must be made, yes or no. In the workplace, the discernment to suffer the consequences of aggressive competition could mean the sacrifice of a career so that one asks for the rest of one's life, what if I had fought for my rights, what if, what if? Whatever it means, we must assert that this discernment presides over the destruction of something beautiful. It is the wanton ruin of the work of nature and culture to be despised every bit as much as the crudest sacrilege. The most beautiful thing in the world was crushed on Calvary. And the suffering and the loss goes on. No consideration of even the resurrection can assuage this agony, make it go away, or blot out its memory. Yet because of the hope that lies beyond it, we can trust that God will bring out of it a good that will take away its sting and its sense of despair. Therefore, we cannot hang back from urging a person to go through the veil, if we believe in them and in the grace of their lives.

It probably doesn't even need to be said, but persecution of this kind, and the decision not to run away from it, is to join in solidarity with the poor and oppressed of our world, which make up a big percent of the world's population. Economically starved, culturally deprived, they drink their cup to the dregs thanks to television which, viewed in hovels with dirt floors and no running water shows them what they don't have and can't get to. What a few persons do, in choosing to suffer for righteousness' sake, is to lift the burden of the world off of the poor for even an instant. They allow something else, something good to happen that pulls back, even momentarily, the dark curtain of fear and oppression. The wholesome light which they admit is incalculable.

Having considered the fifth step from the director's point of view, it remains to reflect a bit on the situation of the persecuted. The direst weapon of the violent person is the sense of shame they inflict, along with the pain. What gets communicated, and is sometimes even verbalized, in the attack, is the loathing the attacker feels for the victim. The attacked person must suffer this knowledge that someone else hates them. A greater diminishment cannot be imagined, especially because the kind of attacks we have in mind here come from those we trusted or knew intimately. The cold and bitter wound is that someone with whom we have been closely associated has harbored these feelings against us and they have finally been made known. There may be explanations; mental disorders may be diagnosed; plausible reasons for the behavior can be discovered. But the victim must live with the fact of a broken world where injustice reigns, and that at very close quarters. One can never be the same afterwards.

The temptation of the persecuted is to think that there is something wrong with himself. To deepen and mature a world view of someone who looks upon the world as basically a blessed place, who has had no reason to doubt the essential love of parents and family, and who is accustomed to the interior journey of self-knowledge, does not happen overnight. One does not learn immediately to be shrewd as a serpent in sizing up peoples' motives. To be sure, one knows about human treachery and vile behavior, but this only on the periphery of one's life, or in books. But when the evil violates him when he is about to harvest his own garden after a lifetime of received nourishment, then the trauma is acute. Having no experience of resisting such abuse, the person absorbs it into his own frame. The person has not yet learned how to resist it. A fragile structure will weaken and eventually collapse and the cycle of abuse will include yet another abuser. A stalwart structure needs advice. Therefore, the director's responsibility is to help the person discern his own behavior as well as the attacker's. Though he may love the attacker, he cannot be drawn into a blindness that refuses to look at the hate and the violence. One has to name the monster for what it is, and not fall into the trap of self-doubt or weak dependency. If this discernment is not made correctly, then the pattern of abuse will simply repeat itself over again.

In a monastic community, a correct discernment may lead to an intervention against a sick member whom the community deems indispensable. The temptation on the part of all is to go soft and so miss the opportunity to save the sick one. Frequently, an initial intervention is made, found to be messy and never repeated. If the process of healing is going to be fruitful, it has to be reapplied time and again. There must be commitment and stability even here in the therapeutic stage. In a marriage, it could mean separation or the taking of a strong position opposing certain types of behavior. In the workplace, it may mean running the risk of getting fired or losing the confidence and taking the anger of the authorities. Whatever the case, one cannot and should not arrive at such a discernment without careful consultation with a trusted advisor or guide.

Rebuilding a Life on the Promised Land

After the long struggle to live according to the gospel, even in the ruin of what we once thought was the fine life we had made for ourselves, we look around us and our situation. We look at the land on which we live. We must begin anew. We cling to the land as to a mother. The land gifts us with a variety of good things: laughing and crying; the change of seasons, and above all, the gradual immersion in a community of like-minded persons. Now that we have made clear to the group who we are and what we stand for, community can once again be salutary. The feminine nurturing qualities of the land are unmistakable. Many monks use the analogy of family and hearth to help them articulate the experience. Yet as soon as stability on the land feeds the now maturer energies, another kind of yearning emerges in the heart—the yearning for a home of another dimension. The quest for an ideal place of peace and rest; the love of a trusting woman, and a home so entirely one's own that it feels like a longing for childhood, are masculine in character. Obviously, imagery of this sort can apply to monks only; nuns have a whole different set of perceptions and images. Often, the yearning for one's childhood home and the nostalgia for an innocence that is forever shattered, cannot be separated from the more spiritual desires. Yet, nostalgia for God is born of the very human loneliness most deeply experienced on empty Sunday afternoons. After looking over the land in our lonely leisure, we return to Vespers with its messianic psalms singing of the mystery of Christ in which the two sides of our human nature are contained. The settled, agricultural and urban character of the wisdom books of the Hebrew Testament contrast with the dynamic, restless tone of the Exodus and conquest narratives. Both are necessary aspects of the Promised Land. The one gives rise to the other, in the manner of mutual enrichment. The growth, purpose and order of the land, having gone through its own kind of Red Sea experience, allow the leisure for the quest and the misery of longing. The nurturing qualities of the land heighten the capacity for dreaming and speculation—that is, for energy and adventure. The more one harvests, the less one seems to have, because one's horizons are always widening. New dimensions seem not just possible, but agonizingly imperative. Walter Brueggemann shows the intertwining relationship of the two sides of the Promised Land when he writes: "Land is always fully historical but always the bearer of over-pluses of meaning known only to those who lose and yearn for it."[2]

Stability on the land where we have suffered increases self-awareness and self-knowledge. The terrible realization of our own unworthiness before God spurs us on to a greater fidelity. We yearn for the innocence of God, and we can have no rest until we move towards it. Yet we could never grow to this dimension without the healing and nurturing qualities of the land. In fact, it is through the land that Christ makes his move towards us in healing. We cannot enjoy communion with God without first having our issues anointed with oil and our wounds bound with clean bandages. Nor can we afford to let down our defenses before God's medicinal approach until we are strong enough for the encounter. God's prevenient healing waters our land while we are stable there, in order to enable us to move on towards a meeting with him in a land we do not yet know. The Promised Land, therefore, has both stability and mobility as its energies. All the riches of the culture of talents and the development of the virtues give rise to the adventurous quest for the beyond and the not-yet. Having learned to love Christ in his teaching on suffering for righteousness' sake, we can yearn for that final dwelling with the transcendent, Trinitarian God: "Those who love me will keep my word, and my Father will love them, and we will come to them and make our home with them" (John 14:23). So our home, our land, becomes ". . . a place well-filled with memories of life with him and promises from him and vows to him."[3]

[2] Ibid., 3.
[3] Ibid., 6.

The Exterior and Interior Landscape

When the role of spiritual director passes to a trusted friend, with whom we can share the most intimate feelings and observations, then we begin to see things with new eyes. The creation takes on deeper colors, brighter aspects. It has become a new creation, after the sufferings, death and resurrection of step four. Our passover of suffering, especially when it comes in the middle years, grants us a vision very like that of the man born blind who receives the gift of sight for the first time when Jesus anoints him with the new creation of dust and spittle. The healing which this vision represents, however, is generally accompanied by a friend, through whom, partly, at any rate, we are raised up. The friend helps to interpret for us those things on the land which we are seeing now and have never seen before.

Spiritual intimacy with a friend presupposes relational maturity that has passed beyond selfishness. Curiosity, intrigue and openness characterize every human encounter, especially the encounters at depth. Moving from self-preoccupation to the perception of a larger world where the spiritual journey of others, and of all others, is important, we also behold the performance of the natural world as it enfolds to our larger senses all the intricacies which have so beguiled human beings from the beginning. Things that pass with the seasons, ephemeral, to be sure, also sink roots in eternity. The daily dance of mists, stars, vistas on the horizon of orange and blue, sunlight falling dappled on the silk of things, all paint images of salvation, grace and holiness on a mind thirsting for God and God's ways. The leisure to share this longing with another grants also the vision to notice the permanent hold on beauty which the bird possesses fluttering over a bush. In the same way, one also awakens to the story that a farm, a ranch or a plantation has locked up in itself where history has long dwelt. Eyes see down and wide with acuity. And they understand. Looking at nature, with possibilities of philosophy and theology is the vocation of writers such as Barry Lopez:

> If you walk up, say, a dry arroyo in the Sonoran Desert, you will feel a mounding and rolling of sand and silt beneath your

foot that is distinctive. You will anticipate the crumbling of the
sedimentary earth in the arroyo bank as your hand reaches out,
and in that tangible evidence you will sense a history of water
in the region. Perhaps a black-throated sparrow lands in a
paloverde bush—the resiliency of the twig under the bird, that
precise shade of yellowish-green against the milk-blue sky, the
fluttering whir of the arriving sparrow, are what I mean by
"landscape". . . .[4]

The land has a history as well as a constantly shimmering
present. The story of a land can be known historically. But it
can come alive through empathy with the misfortunes or the
happiness of those who lived there. It becomes the object of
contemplation only when we have crossed the threshold of the
paschal mystery and walk the land as the new creation which
groans inwardly until the revelation of the children of God. As
such, our praise of God on the land finds its expression not
just on the sunny spring days, when all creation rings out its
joy, but also through ugly weather, storms, wind, and hail
which destroy crops and blow birds' nests away. The contemplation, too, of a praying mantis with a festooned caterpillar in
its forepaws, takes on aspects that are dark and deadly. Christ
underwent suffering for our sakes. Being veterans ourselves,
we are never far from the suffering of the oppressed. Rooted
in the land, with all its destructive tendencies, we know the
oppression of the innocent who may have lived on this land
before us. Do we live on fields where slaves once toiled? If so,
we endure the hopeless wailing of the tortured and the exiled.
Do we live where Native Americans left tools behind them, to-
kens of their presence, mercilessly banished by the European
settlers? Can we experience the confusion of uprooted peoples
who doubt the benignity and providence of God? In the matrix of clouds and darkness, with scurrying greyness rushing
over our heads somewhere towards a new feast of rape, Truth
lays its tranquil eggs in the heart and covers them over with
strength for pain. Later, on a child's day of choice, through
many full moons of peace, Truth will hatch its young for

---

[4] Barry Lopez, "Landscape and Narrative," *Crossing Open Ground*
(New York: Scribner's, 1988) 61–71.

growth and wisdom. The land on which we live, well interpreted by a friend and guide, will grow quiet with its history,
for good or for ill. But it will always remember what went on
there. Anyone who chooses to live on the land, is invited to
live with its history, in such a way as to expiate and redeem it
in one's own transformation in Christ.

The fourth step of humility, and the concomitant fifth step,
by which a guide helps us to interpret what has happened to
us, now effects a transformation on the interior landscape, our
spiritual land or home where we dwell with God. It is nothing
less than the beginnings of an integration which marries
within us earth and heaven, making the two one. Barry Lopez
speaks of the marriage in this way:

> [The interior landscape is] a kind of projection within a person
> of a part of the exterior landscape. Relationships in the exterior
> landscape include those that have names and are discernible,
> such as the nitrogen cycle, or a vertical sequence of ordovician
> limestone, and others that are unmodified or ineffable, such as
> winter light falling on a particular kind of granite, or the effect
> of humidity on the frequency of a blackpoll warbler's song.
> That these relationships have purpose and order, however in-
> scrutable they may seem to us, is a tenet of evolution. Similarly,
> the speculations, intuitions, and formal ideas we refer to as
> "Mind" are a set of relationships in the interior landscape with
> purpose and order; some of these are obvious, many impene-
> trably subtle. The shape and character of these relationships in
> a person's thinking, I believe, are deeply influenced by where
> on this earth one goes, what one touches, the patterns one ob-
> serves in nature—the intricate history of one's life in the land,
> even a life in the city, where wind, the chirp of birds, the line of
> a falling leaf, are known. These thoughts are arranged further,
> according to the thread of one's moral, intellectual, and spirit-
> ual development. The interior landscape responds to the char-
> acter and subtlety of an exterior landscape; the shape of the
> individual mind is affected by land as it is by genes.[5]

The monastic life forms our interior horizons by its own
program of conversion to Christ. But because it insists on stability in the community, or, for those who live outside a

[5] Ibid., 65.

monastery, on stability in a lived situation, the interior cannot help but be affected by the exterior. The complex set of relationships between the moral, spiritual and intellectual elements of our interior, gradually meld with grass, the birds, the buildings and even the street where we live. Learning to love the new creation of Christ's abiding, demands that we notice the smallest detail on the snails beneath our feet. Their specificity becomes as dear to us, as compelling, as the greatest intentions for which we pray. "Whoever is faithful in a very little is faithful also in much; and whoever is dishonest in a very little is dishonest also in much" (Luke 16:10). Somehow, the very insignificance of the external geography, when it is known and loved, allows the spirit to penetrate to that plane where all things human and humanized converge. Though it is often inarticulate, because it is so riddled with stops and starts, the gradual sewing of the exterior landscape with the interior one, is one of the chief works of the monastic.

Steps Six, Seven and Eight: RB 7.49-55

[49]The sixth step of humility is that a monk is content with the lowest and most menial treatment, and regards himself as a poor and worthless workman in whatever task he is given, [50]saying to himself with the Prophet: *I am insignificant and ignorant, no better than a beast before you, yet I am with you always* (Ps 72[73]:22-23).

[51]The seventh step of humility is that a man not only admits with his tongue but is also convinced in his heart that he is inferior to all and of less value, [52]humbling himself and saying with the Prophet: *I am truly a worm, not a man, scorned by men and despised by the people* (Ps 21[22]:7). [53]*I was exalted, then I was humbled and overwhelmed with confusion* (Ps 87[88]:16). [54]And again, *It is a blessing that you have humbled me so that I can learn your commandments* (Ps 118[119]:71,73).

[55]The eighth step of humility is that a monk does only what is endorsed by the common rule of the monastery and the example set by his superiors.

•••

Only a light commentary is necessary here, not because of the strangeness of the subject matter for people of our time, but because of the gossamer quality of the virtue of hope to which they point. When the exterior and the interior landscapes begin to meld, as we have seen in the previous steps, the weight of the here and now, appreciated more than ever before, paradoxically becomes less. It is easier to let go of. Do we become more mobile, because we are more rooted? Is our hope more elastic, stretching into realms hitherto unsuspected?

Step 6: How is it that the Rule can speak of the poorest and the worst of everything, now, when our appreciation of everything has increased? The answer lies not in our attitude toward things, but in the attitude of the community or our peers toward us. We are no longer young and exciting. The fascination with us is gone. The arc which our trajectory traced from early development, fecundity and zenith of our physical and mental powers, to say nothing of our imaginative forces, is now on the backslide. Not scorn, but neglect, not loss of respect but abandonment is our lot. If we have never tasted it before, we have now to swallow the Lord's words: "Prophets are not without honor except in their own country and in their own house" (Matt 13:57).

Where I once boasted, though modestly, of course, about my former skill in classical languages, in my exploits in carpentry, my dates with the rich and famous, as any one who has had a career will do, I now appreciate and adopt a reserve. Since I am not playing the game the others are, they ignore me, think me gone dry, or out of step. How can I boast of what I have been through? Or do I hang my spiritual trophies on a wall for all to comment upon? Instead, I must be content with the polite dismissal of the me who used to be, when my fur was shiny, when I was the center of attention. For a sophisticated person, at least, this is the most menial treatment imaginable.

Step 7: In the growth of self-knowledge and in the appreciation of my neighbor, especially in the admittance to my heart of mature friends, I can actually consider myself less than most others. Having arrived at that place where I know my neighbor's struggle, and habitually consider her moral achievements over and above my own, I acknowledge myself less than her and inferior to most. My aggressive and competitive days are over. For me, this is no longer an humiliation but an accepted fact with which I am comfortable. If I can not openly proclaim "I am a worm and no man," at least it is not as outrageous a thought as it used to be.

When this new situation starts to make itself known and felt, my claw hold on any place I once called home is loosened. I can afford to dream and speculate about another home. Having moved off from faith, my hope takes on more spiritual characteristics, more ardent desire. Values have changed and are likely to keep changing. This is no longer a threat to one who is no longer entrenched in certain customs and thought patterns. In my own new freedom, I can respect and admire the free behavior of others.

Consider the doctrine in RB 57.1-3: "If there are artisans in the monastery, they are to practice their craft with all humility . . . If the artisan becomes puffed up by his skillfulness in his craft, and feels that he is conferring something on the monastery, he is to be removed from practicing his craft. . . ." This now gets transformed into lasting virtue, since what I do, while it is still all for the community, is no longer part of my persona which I must defend against all comers, and constantly declare its value. And when I choose not to protect myself by pride, then humility is my gift, freely and abundantly bestowed by the people with whom I live.

Step 8: When a monastic has arrived at this stage, close to God though she is, she nevertheless will have bouts of doubt about the utter helplessness of her stance of no defense. When she is tempted to stand up for her rights, or, more subtly, to have things the way they used to be, she is well reminded of the eighth step, that a nun should never do anything out of the ordinary, that is, never call attention to herself by any extraordinary activity. The eighth step does not come naturally to young people or newcomers. It is the preserve of the holy veterans.

Acutely aware of the whole silent drama being played out in her life, the nun would never do anything to call attention to herself, for fear that the promised land she can already taste and see from a distance will evaporate if she reaches out to grab it. Possessed of exquisite knowledge, but not yet possessing love, she keeps strong her doctrine of reserve. She does not throw "her pearls before swine" (Matt 7:6).

The middle steps of humility indicate how a life lived on the land of one's given situation can lead us on a journey that mysteriously remains rooted in promises and commitments. The journey is through faith to hope, and the happiness which the promise holds out to us. In our post-Christian society, we can no longer depend on our culture to tell us what is changing and what is permanent. Religious faith alone can tell us that. People coming from a society of rapid change, come to us with questions. We can understand their questions by our very reflection on the constant change of things, ourselves and our landscapes. People come to us weary of change, and weary of a society which can no longer force permanence on marriage or on any other institution. But people are also wary of any institution which demands lifetime commitment. Monasticism seems to many to be outrageous in its focus on permanent commitment to God. The irony is that no one can make commitment to God in the monastery, without first knowing the quintessential character of change inherent in all creation, including ourselves. The monastic tradition abides in one place in order to go on a journey to another. It thereby discovers a new content to the land where it is stable, and a different kind of commitment based on faith in God who gives a participation in his own life as the means to make the metaphysical voyage from faith to hope and, finally, to love.

> If you want to change,
> Stand still.
> If you want to grow
> Get rooted.
> Wandering around without growth,
> Reproducing the easy green shoots without blooms
> Creating compulsively, self-consciously
> Smothers everything

Even the wonders of the world
With sameness.

If you want to improve,
Practice.
If you want people to listen to your song,
Work.
Work like the bird who wakes before dawn
To improve his song.
The one who sings the best
Gets the mate.
The one who gets the mate
Has something to sing about.

Prepare the hour
When the flower blooms
And the fruit swells,
When the flower pries open its petals
And the dew on the petals are tears,
When the fruit ripens, dropping away
And ripping the lamenting wood.

You have only one hour, one showing,
But a lifetime of swelling
Till the term closes and the season sells out.

You have only one way,
Narrow and straight,
Though your load weighs on the knees at the needle.

Abide, remain, proceed, advance,
Forgetting what lies behind except sin,
Till your body bows Eucharistic
On the cross.

CHAPTER SIX

A Marginal Place:
The Steps of Humility 9–12

The passage from the Desert to the Garden is not so much a "translocation" as it is a "transformation" of the same turf. The Promised Land, however, represents neither passage nor stability, but rather, hope—a hope for a place that is not yet known. Having left the society and the spirit of the age, but not yet having arrived at the goal of the kingdom of God, the monk finds himself in a kind of limbo. He belongs no longer here, yet he is not yet there. The hundredfold reward which Jesus promised is his, to be sure: "Truly I tell you, there is no one who has left house or brothers or sisters or mother or father or children or fields, for my sake and for the sake of the good news, who will not receive a hundredfold now in this age—houses, brothers and sisters, mothers and children, and fields, with persecutions—and in the age to come eternal life" (Mark 10:29-30).

Yet what quality will the "hundredfold in this age" possess? Having renounced these things, with what kind of hands will the monk receive them again? The answer can only be: with hands which "buy as though they had no possessions" (1 Cor 7:30). That kind of behavior, which we may consider a *terminus* in itself, between the spirit of renunciation and the joy of full spiritual possession, we call "marginal."

The Marginality of the Monastic Community

Some persons are marginalized by a society economically, socially, racially or in some other way. If one does not band together with other marginalized persons to form a minority, one dies. Hagar, having been put away by Abraham, wandered about in the wilderness. But for God's intervention, she would have perished. As she sat opposite her child, "she lifted up her voice and wept. And God heard the voice of the boy . . ." (Gen 21:16-17).

Similarly, the scapegoat is sent into the wilderness, not as a sacrifice for sin, but for the exile of the people's sins to the demon, Azazel, in the desert. Even the man who leads out the goat from the camp, must wash his clothes before returning. We cannot survive without belonging somehow to a group and accepting its terms. Monastic life leads a person from the midst of society to its perimeter. Such a voluntary marginalization would seem to be independent of traditional exile, and might be strong in its own righteousness, not needing assistance. Yet monastics have found that the support of like-minded individuals is imperative if spiritual renunciation wants to be fruitful. Likewise, if one were somehow to live a comprehensive monastic discipline while remaining in the society, that person would probably be ostracized in some way by those around him. Therefore, such persons need the networking support of a loving community made possible in our culture today by phone, frequent traveling, computer modems and other such media. Still, life on the perimeter or in an anonymous urban setting remains difficult, even with a supportive community. Let none of us take it upon ourselves without firm and mature deliberation.

When persons are marginalized in a search for goodness, they become prophets for the society which they have forsaken (or by which they have been forsaken) in one of three ways. Either they remove themselves out of criticism and in protest of the society's values, or they seek to uncover a real but neglected dimension of the human person. This latter way is, in some sense, a criticism, but its direction is taken up by the search for wisdom and not by the spirit of judgment. A third way of prophecy, of course, is involuntary exile where the society has ostracized people for the wrong reason. In each of these cases, prophecy is inevitable for the justified, marginalized group, because it has gone out of the home community for the sake of values that transcend the home community. The motives for voluntary marginalization must be fundamentally pure, for the minority community cannot survive without prophetic reference to the home community. Even if the exiles have been driven out from their home, they cannot survive unless their marginalization is rooted in justice. Willful separation for impure reasons can only feed on bitterness. It can only wither and die. But if marginalization is sincere and good, prophecy arises to feed off unseen nourishment that exile has discovered. In solitude, the prophet has identified values to which the society is blind or against which it has turned a deaf ear. A corrective voice within or without the society cries out to right the current wrong or fill the present lack. Prophecy is no less important because of its sponsor than because of the message itself. To whom does the prophet point? Whose word is it that the prophet speaks? Every society would do well to listen to its authentically marginalized peoples in order to hear the message that comes to it from beyond itself. And if one can identify a transcendent providence, then one can also affirm its presence at the very heart of society, even though it can be seen only from the margin. The heartaches and the true inner needs of a society are to be found in the cries and laments of those on the periphery.

What Marginality Is Not

In current monastic jargon, the term, "marginal," has pejorative overtones. If one is marginal in a monastic community, one might as well return to the world. To be marginal within a marginal community is to be nothing at all. For one is neither cold nor hot. Unless one is speaking of a double prophecy, against the exiled community as well as the home community, a second marginalization is meaningless. For one is denying the very reason for the marginality, namely, the prophecy of the marginal community. Monastics receive support from one another when they keep close to the center of the goodness and righteousness which originally lured them into their exile. Here we come close to the dynamics of a Christian monastic community, separated from the world, yet joined to its very heart in mystery. For marginalization is most fully realized in all its positive aspects in Christ and his Body. One is called apart to the monastic community by Christ, to whom we adhere; without whom we are the most abject of persons. Once the value of separation from the world and adherence to Christ is announced and embraced in the heart, one must run with Christ with all force. Any deviation from the race is deadly. "Whoever is not with me is against me, and whoever does not gather with me scatters. Therefore I tell you, people will be forgiven for every sin and blasphemy, but blasphemy against the Spirit will not be forgiven" (Matt 12:30-31).

To lose momentum, or even to slip out of the circle of Christ is to lose all centripetal force. One becomes a nonentity, floating into outer space in an atmosphere without oxygen and without definition. Therefore, we must distinguish carefully between marginalization as an essential part of the monastic program, and that self-defeating separation called lukewarmness, which denies the Holy Spirit as well as the human spirit. Since the term "marginal" has acquired new meaning in world philosophy and economics, it seemed better to retain it and gain from it, and to run the risk of confusion with its pejorative, religious sense.

Personal Marginality

How does the monastic experience this marginality? How does one personally interiorize it? The answer lies in how the monastic bridges the chasm between the hundredfold reward in this age, and the kingdom of God to which the hundredfold reward points. In what sense do we understand these "houses and brothers and sisters and fathers and mothers, children, and fields" which constitute the hundredfold reward? In a sense that transcends these categories of ours.

First of all, renunciation of family and friends produces a heightened awareness of both their goodness and their cruelty in our lives. Their fullness and their inadequacy can now be acknowledged on a level which allows growth to take place in us. We can assume the good we received from them, and we can begin to deal with the bad. We shall always have a relationship with them, for we are never meant to be cut off from them; we are called to affirm the relationship at the level of Christ. "For whoever does the will of my Father in heaven is my brother and sister and mother" (Matt 12:50).

Our mothers and fathers, brothers and sisters are now liberated from any negativity which the emotional web of family and friends may have spun around us.[1] At the same time, we add on the new family which the monastery provides—a family based on the kingdom of God. In a very real way, the nurturing and support of a family becomes very richly operative during our journey to God in the midst of a believing community. There is of course always the possibility of some negativity here, some dysfunctional dependency and manipulation, but the thrust of the monastic life militates against such evil, and allows the inherent goodness of mothering and fathering to assume its fullest meaning. When the kingdom of God is present in the monastery, we experience an abundance of mothers, fathers, sisters and brothers, lands and everything else which Jesus described as the hundredfold reward.

Not only family and friends, but also career, skills and art come under the rule of renunciation. These, too, the monk receives back a hundredfold. A mature monk can often say, "I am much more of a painter/scholar/carpenter/sculptor/ manager now than I ever would have been had I not come to the monastery." The new monk needs to hear this when, in the crisis of self-identity, he feels the loss of equilibrium due to his inactivity as an artist or artisan or scholar. The dilemma which faces the newcomer is acute. For what remains truly a part of his heart, even after monastic entrance and renunciation, must

---

[1] For a good overview of family systems theory, see Michael E. Kerr and Murray Bowen, *Family Evaluation: An Approach Based on Bowen Theory* (New York and London: Norton, 1988); see also Edwin H. Friedman, *Generation to Generation: Family Process in Church and Synagogue* (New York and London: Guilford Press, 1985).

be remade along monastic lines. Monastic tradition knows this to be an arduous and bitter process. But there is great joy, also, as the monk feels the liberation from aggressive professionalism and its narrow, provincial concerns. One no longer has to live a career or conform to standards erected by current fickle tastes. The monk can afford to put out to sea with open imagination. He can utilize whatever discipline he had learned as a means for art, but he is not thereby limited to it. He is limited only by the demands of truth, beauty, and timeless good taste. Outside the track of a professional career, his dimensions are wider, his horizons broader. He can now push out at the boundaries of what is known. He can become a dreamer. Not confined to the approval of a public, he can afford to take chances.

What keeps the serious monastic artisan, or artist or scholar supple to the Spirit is the willingness to apply again and again the first renunciation. By doing this, one also enjoys time after time the taste of first freedom. This freedom of the heart, always available, keeps the will from taking back any part of an old identity. The tendency to do so, however, is ever present, since every trial forces the person to look to the old ways for assurance and consolation. The monastic artisan might even be producing good work, but outside the monastic discipline. And so the ultimate fruit in his own life will be bad. And his consequent behavior, full of the bad fruit of his heart, will cause great suffering to those around him. No human product justifies an unclean heart. In the kingdom of God, even apparently good things must be foregone if Christ is offering the human person something better.

Hence, the monastic faces the challenge of voluntarily separating from the practice of a craft or a project, or submitting to the wise direction of a senior. At the same time, prudence dictates that one must at the same time provide outlets for one's legitimate expressive needs. When the monastic is permitted or decides to take up again the craft or science, according to a slow pace discerned in the light of the Holy Spirit, one accepts the fact that one is working for no one but God and the human family. The taste of it is sweeter than honey in the mouth. One should not cling to the richness of it, but rather should buy with one's treasure the whole field of God's peace, beauty and truth. Monastics wonder at how much God wills to pour into them. They understand that the hundredfold reward is but an Hebraism for incalculable pleasure: "Give, and it will be given to you. A good measure, pressed down, shaken together, running over, will be put into your lap; for the measure you give will be the measure you get back" (Luke 6:38).

The secret is the willingness to remain marginal with one's skill, enjoying it and God to the full, but accepting a place on the periphery where it remains hidden from the calculation of one's contemporaries. Nevertheless, the monastic assumes the role of a prophet for any skill one represents. One's own freedom and the skeins of imagination that are woven on the skyline, get cartooned back into the world's art and skill, according to the mysterious plan of Christ. The monastic, in his or her own limited way, produces art for art's sake, that is, for Christ's, without restraint of career considerations and without reference to the taboos of the current epoch. To remain free from the lure of career and the approval of others, and to seek insignificance in solitude and especially in silence is the only appropriate stance for a monastic.

Steps Nine, Ten and Eleven: RB 7.56-61

[56]The ninth step of humility is that a monk controls his tongue and remains silent, not speaking unless asked a question, [57]for Scripture warns, *In a flood of words you will not avoid sinning* (Pro 10:19), [58]and, *A talkative man goes about aimlessly on earth* (Ps 139[140]:12).

[59]The tenth step of humility is that he is not given to ready laughter, for it is written: *Only a fool raises his voice in laughter* (Sir 21:23).

[60]The eleventh step of humility is that a monk speaks gently and without laughter, seriously and with becoming modesty, briefly and reasonably, but without raising his voice, [61]as it is written: "A wise man is known by his few words."

•••

Silence can mean many things. Even the silence enjoined by the Rule signifies different interior attitudes, depending on where the monk is on the spiritual journey. Most would agree that monastic silence is first and foremost a discipline to be observed. Such it is for the first stage of the spiritual life as we have outlined it in this book. The first step of humility presupposes the discipline of silence as a cardinal means of vigilance over the monk's compulsive reactions and relational needs. Only by that vigilance can the doorway to the interior landscape be discovered.

Our culture offers precious little to support such an idea. We have made a heavy investment in the belief of the sovereignty of the individual, over against the legitimate demands of society and community. We do not feel comfortable in a group until we have made our own unique contribution, usually by the spoken word. The ethos of the time, and our understanding of the human person encourage us to do so. We self-authenticate by our contribution to the group spoken in an egalitarian atmosphere. Not much stock is given to the precept: "Speaking and teaching are the master's task; the disciple is to be silent and listen" (RB 6.6).

That we have incorporated into our daily lifestyle an easy flow of words is evident from the mass communication media. Talk shows abound on radios; music fills every waiting room and office. Radios, sound systems and amplification, to say nothing of television, invade every quiet place we are likely to encounter during the day. Our technology abhors silence, yet how appreciative we become when we experience a drop of it. Even the content of the talk shows corroborates this all pervasive tendency to self-authenticate by speech. We are fascinated by ourselves, and our stories, no matter how banal. Persons who can hardly speak a language make up the lion's portion of such entertainment. But, apparently, they remind us of ourselves, and make self-authentication easier as we identify with the personages on the screen or at the microphone.

There is a subtle cheat going on here. The more we have championed individuality, the more egalitarian we become, the more we have levelled ourselves to a depleted sameness. The hard work of individuality is too demanding for most of us. We would gladly prefer to let someone on the television do it for us. Hence we are witnessing the mind drain on a massive scale in the less educated segments of our population. And this portion of the populace is growing all the time, as people revert less and less to the mind and more and more to a caricature of it. The more we retreat from healthy liberal arts programs in our universities, and the more we cater to the demand for technical and business courses that supposedly insure employment, the more our entire educational system plays into the hands of the mass media. Ironically, the more individualistic we seem, the more similar we have actually become. By means of a few television shows, the whole nation, and, indeed, many parts of the world, view the same propaganda and, like the children behind the Pied Piper, begin to think the same, and adopt the same fashions and attitudes. And this sameness is conveyed most tellingly by the sameness of constant speech. The balance of silence is never allowed to pour its own content from other realms of the imagination into our present discourse.

Monastics cannot escape this societal reality. Newcomers to our monasteries today want and need to talk more than former generations. Silence as a discipline comes hard and seems so foreign. Adopted for a few days out of zeal for the good, the observance is quickly abandoned as the monastic seeks to find entry into the easy comfort level of the community. It is openly admitted that we enjoy far less silence today in our monasteries than we had in the past. Yet, the tradition of silence cannot just evaporate. It continues to stand by with its goods for sale, confident that one day its ways will be popular again. The structures of the monastery ensure a certain amount of silence, such as the so-called Grand Silence, when speaking is discouraged toward the time of retirement in the evening until the liturgy of the morning hours is completed. But traditional monastic strictures against talking are meant to be applied best precisely during the work day. In today's communities, the work place and all such community gatherings have become a focal point of verbal communication. All across the monastic world, concern has risen high over the demise of the practice of silence, and the reluctance to return to the artificiality of sign making and strict physical boundaries to avoid speaking.

In the meantime, the nun makes progress in her community to the point that the stage of "striving" passes into the stage of "proceeding." The vigilance that was first inspired, at least in part, by the desire to conform to the Rule in order to please a demanding God and to win the favor of the authorities of the community, now becomes more and more a constant prayer of the heart to a loving God and an energized service of the neighbors she lives with. Little time is wasted. Personal needs are reduced to a minimum. The long years of formation to silence and solitude have led to a self-knowledge which has honed her relational skills so that people seek her out. She has found within herself a place of compassion. Others come near to enjoy the neutral space she offers where there is no judgment, only affirmation and a place to unfold and relax. Words and communication reach their ripening point. They are heavy with nourishing meaning for others. They contain a nectar of life so concentrated as to taste far more potent than one would expect from their outward appearance. People come to gather more of it. The more she exercises this in-house ministry, the more the Holy Spirit seems to demand it of her, so that it becomes an imperative in her spiritual life. Time takes on a more sacral character as the moments of the day assume a value as precious as pearls wet from the creator's hand. Moments of silence and solitude, either at the beginning of the day when it is still dark, or at the time of repose at night, seem like an oasis in the desert. She waits for them like the return of a long-lost friend and their reunion is sweet and comforting. The nourishment of this meeting is her daily bread. Like the manna in the desert, it is just enough to depress her hunger so that she can continue her journey, yet it leaves her unsatisfied and quickens her step for the next meeting point to which her constant hope leads her.

We must now consider silence and solitude in the life of this nun as a welcome balance to the activities of the day. Far from being a discipline as they formerly were, the exercise of silence and solitude grows into a privilege she dare not ask for, but which she eagerly seizes when it is given. No one has to remind her of their value. No one has to encourage her to take time for herself. From being passive to the impossible demands of silence and solitude, she is now active in their pursuit. She can afford to examine all their intricacies, all their hidden parts, especially as she finds them in the Rule: that one should refrain from even good words; that one should say little or nothing until one is approached or asked a question; that laughter should be only lightly indulged in; and that all her speech be modest. She studies these things; she corroborates them, and, in silence, enjoys the wisdom of the ancients.

From the stage of "proceeding," the nun passes slowly to the entry way of "fulfillment." She allows the Holy Spirit to inspire her with that most difficult Benedictine discernment, the restraint of even good words. The Rule, quoting the psalmist, declares: "I was silent and was humbled, and I refrained even from good words" (Ps 38[19]:2-3).

At first tentatively, and then, more frequently, the monk finds himself more engaged with the truth of things, persons and situations. Less and less self-referenced, minimally concerned about what any particular action will mean for him, how he will look, and what others will think, he is captivated by the workings of God in all events. He notices the moral implications of behavior and how everything enters the struggle between good and evil. As such, he prays constantly for light in his every involvement, his every thought. His vigilance now becomes a way of life inseparable from his mode of acting and representing his very being. The early steps of humility claim their fulfillment in this stage, because their injunctions are so interiorized so as to never be mentioned, but taken for granted in a kind of permanent structure of the mind and heart. Ever ready for adversity and hardship, the monk also embraces quietly the lean times and the frustration of adversity predicted by step four. Humility gains the status of a habit in him, so that his outlook toward others is unselfconscious, or nearly so. Not needing speech to validate his own position in any encounter, he now waits for the Spirit to speak in another, or through himself out of silence.

One never refrains from speaking, unless a greater is present and claims precedence which is given by the others out of courtesy. This is the deepest meaning of silence in the Rule, a silence which allows God to speak because he is so near.

Where the monk is, no matter what he is doing, God is present with a saving intention. God's approach is always with love, interest, and the desire to be engaged in what the monk is doing. The monk responds by recognizing the sacred character of the moment, of every moment, just as the Rule has suggested by the phrase, *omni hora*. A deference to the other, especially to God; a control over levity, except when lovingly appropriate; and the ability to articulate a message in wise, plain and simple language—these are the guarantees that silence has entered the monk's heart in a transformational way and awakened there a love that can only be expressed non verbally. For love is action for God, possession of God, the willingness to be acted upon by God with the confidence that God will do no injury.

Renunciation of speech passes into the eloquence of silence where God speaks in another language heard both in this world and in the more inclusive world of the Realm of God. Our behavior and our silence here seem like an exile and a marginalization. And for many of our contemporaries, that is precisely what they are. But this silence has identified a richer content to the ephemeral world of easy speech and casual acquaintance. These surface realities suddenly stand revealed as the holy means, when purified, of sacred encounter where human beings, and, indeed, the whole creation with which we come in contact, are called into more significant life and love. We unlock new definitions to personhood. We refuse all limitation and set out on the open sea where God plays with our possibilities which he himself has seen since the foundation of the world.

In order to spell out in more detail how one passes into communion with the citizens of another realm, we will examine separately each of the three steps on silence.

Step 9: "When words are many, transgression is not lacking" (Prov 10:19). The silence which prefers to give the word to others has discovered a wisdom not only in the other person, but in oneself as well. The sin which the wise person commits in speaking is the diminishment that comes from refusing to grow. When one thinks that one is a master and, therefore, a teacher, one will expound on a subject intent only on getting out a circumscribed and limited piece of information. The mistake is not in the teaching, but in the thinking that one is a master. That epithet cannot be given to oneself. It can only be given by others who identify something in us which we are not supposed to be aware of. We will use the field of music to illustrate the point. The master musician, for example, knows what he does not know. He has determined what the whole gamut of music is; that a vast field lies before him; that, of himself, even in a lifetime, he could not learn everything there is to learn about this most exalted human enterprise. But he opens wide his arms to try. Somewhere in the attempt, his being has been opened sufficiently, and with great effort and pain, to embrace both technique and inspiration. When he can hold these two in balance, even though he may not be aware of it, since he is always intent on one or the other, his friends feel the artistry, even while he is caught up in the struggle. Only the audience can bestow the laurels. When the musician is ever a student, when he is forever on the lookout for the gifts which others exhibit in order to further his own search, when he grows silent in order to learn perpetually from others, waiting to find perhaps a better way, never ready to speak unless one queries him, then, in the silence of humility and docility to the gifts of God in other people, he learns true art. Then, he is a master. He has attained this height of awareness only by long training in humility, by the humiliation of having his own efforts corrected and self-corrected time and time again. Vigilance, self-judgment, criticism by others, justified or otherwise, even neglect by contemporaries, forces the artist to yearn for inspiration in the imagining of other worlds from which art comes. Dreaming in sorrow often forces the artist to enrich the content of his own art with the content from the realms of the imagination. In the hands of the artist, our world becomes a larger place. The artist constantly references to places beyond what we can see and touch here.

Step 10: "A fool raises his voice when he laughs" (Sir 21:20). In the growth we experience in the spiritual life, much knowledge is given, and much wisdom. The pain that accompanies growth carries with it an hauteur, a competitive noticing of others, their foibles and their lack of growth. Criticism of others, especially in the form of projection of my own unidentified faults and miseries, frequently takes the form of laughter. Outright sneering is socially unacceptable in most places. But just as much can be accomplished by the subtle put down accompanied by the well-placed snicker. I may even bargain with myself about this, feeling that I should not indulge in ripping someone apart in a conversation behind their back, but I can masquerade my true disdain by cunning laughter. The louder it is, the more I attempt to cover up the depth of my judgment, the more I give myself away. Laughter of this kind is always the flip side of scorn.

In the realm of the sacred, only the most careful words are worthy of speech about another. In the realm of the holy, pure laughter about the predicaments of life carry us forward. Holy laughter indicates a comfort level with myself that is high enough to include others. Together, we can demolish all posturing and break the stuffy silence of false solemnity. But this only occurs by the grace of the Holy Spirit. Laughter can quickly degenerate into a cover up for malice.

Step 11: The eleventh step of humility recommends that a monk speak ". . . gently and without laughter, seriously and with becoming modesty, briefly and reasonably . . ." (RB 7.60). The heart breaking courtesy that the holy monk brings to every encounter assures his gentleness and monastic decorum. But to speak briefly and reasonably belongs to the one whose mind is working to assimilate greater truths that have already been suggested by the conversation. He is still thinking, reflecting. He has no time to pronounce, except on the aspects of the matter that are so obvious as to be almost assumed. And so well digested is his discourse, that he can reduce it to hard and fast articulation, making sure that the nuances are preserved. His thesis will stand up to the most exacting analysis, because it is founded on a clean understanding based on experience as well as reflection. Whether he is learned or not makes no difference. For we are speaking here of knowledge that is sure, based on the workings of a mind that is free, with no persona to protect, with no admixture of emotional states that are out of control, and with the aid of an energy that comes directly from a will on fire with zeal. Behind his few words, therefore, we note a power and a focus that are understandable only to the spiritual guide, but which result in clear statements as eloquent as they are brief and to the point. This does not mean that the monk cannot go on at length. But his speech comes out of a silence that bespeaks an enormous range of emotional, intellectual and intentional activity and which quickly recedes back into a silence which ponders more of the mystery.

Step Twelve: RB 7.62-70

[62]The twelfth step of humility is that a monk always manifests humility in his bearing no less than in his heart, so that it is evident [63]at the Work of God, in the oratory, the monastery or the garden, on a journey or in the field, or anywhere else. Whether he sits, walks or stands, his head must be bowed and his eyes cast down. [64]Judging himself always guilty on account of his sins, he should consider that he is already at the fearful judgment, [65]and constantly say in his heart what the publican in the Gospel said with downcast eyes: *Lord, I am a sinner, not worthy to look up to heaven* (Luke 18:13). [66]And with the Prophet: *I am bowed down and humbled in every way* (Ps 37[38]:7-9; Ps 118[119]:107).

[67]Now, therefore, after ascending all these steps of humility, the monk will quickly arrive at that *perfect love* of God which *casts out fear* (1 John 4:18). [68]Through this love, all that he once performed with dread, he will now begin to observe without effort, as though naturally, from habit, [69]no longer out of fear of hell, but out of love for Christ, good habit and delight in virtue. [70]All this the Lord will by the Holy Spirit graciously manifest in his workman now cleansed of vices and sins.

•••

The interior work in which the monastic has been engaged now begins to manifest itself on the exterior in such a way that even the physical stance and appearance of the person is in conformity to inner attitudes and convictions. The list of seven places where the monastic is observed to be humble symbolizes that one's humble mien is constant and habitual. Almost in apposition to this list is added, "sitting, walking or standing," which crowns the meaning of the list with a trinity of stance and movement. As at the beginning of the steps with the mention of *omni hora*, so also here at the end, St. Benedict proposes a spirituality of continual prayer. What he described as an ideal at the start has, at the finish, turned into a reality. Language, the gateway to the thoughts, has been purified and transformed. Personality has been broken open to the eternal possibilities of the Realm of God. In fact, we can no longer speak of an individual personality, but of God's call to be a fully humanized person in Jesus Christ. Personality is of our making. Personhood is God's summons in love. Human desires and drives for survival, for place, for meaning, have given way to a divinized self united to the Spirit of God, so that the tensions between human and the divine are resolved and further heightened in the paschal mystery of Christ. The glory that Christ knows at the right hand of the Father is now the source and principle of the monastic's being, as the empty vessel of the human heart gets filled with God who created it for this very purpose.

From a region of unlikeness, where the image of God was hidden deep within the retiring human will, to a region of likeness of God, whereby God recognizes and loves the Christ that he sees in the human person, the monastic has travelled all through the vast countryside of the heart, with all its emotional ups and downs, its detours, whether physical, intellectual or moral, and its highways sunken under the sludge of spiritual inertia and fatigue, to the place where everything is in order. One simply comes home. One comes to oneself in an integration of powers and energies that are connected to their source, finally and at the last. In this sense, the monastic becomes nothing more than human, but in the fullest sense of the term—not an angel, not a heavenly being, not a ghost. One comes to the place where Christ is, at the center of the human heart, and from that source, one can feel the power of the risen Christ pulsating through the arteries and the muscles until what was bent over can begin to straighten up and look at the light. Christ alone is the upright one. But now, in our transformation, we, too, can straighten up our backs and rise to our full stature. Having fallen beneath ourselves in sin, having gone off to a distant land and devoured our inheritance from God in debauchery and idolatry, we can now return home fully penitent, and fully forgiven, and take up our rightful duties and privileges as children of God. Being at home with oneself and exercising a self-control that guarantees our freedom carries with it the knowledge of oneself as Christ knows us. We are sinners, but we have been redeemed, and this knowledge acts as a perpetual catalyst which constantly invites us to a higher place at the banqueting table of our own place where God and his Christ have made their home.

The renunciation we practice is of our own idea of things, our own self-validation. And the marginality we receive is God's frequent invitation to come out of ourselves into his glory. These are the visitations of his Word as the Bridegroom of the human heart where love will be celebrated. Far from being a fortress where God cannot penetrate, and far from being the drab personality of routine and schedule, we become constantly open to the greater gift of God's own contemplation of himself in the Trinity. We become passive to God's action, or, rather, we become the place where God is glorified. As such, we stand on the borders of the finite world. We have become truly marginal to all things silly and gross. The whole world, in fact, with all of its petty pursuits, takes on a perspective where God's great movements in the human heart are finally revealed. God's vision of the human heart, not to be separated from his glory, make the passing world look small in comparison. As the heavenly liturgy sounds more and more in the ears of the blessed here on earth, everything seems to get caught up in the rays shining from the wounds of the Lamb. Finally, all is caught up in a single ray of light, which is God himself, and of which the ancients wrote so eloquently to describe the transformation of the world in Christ. Standing at the edge of this shore where this transformation occurs, the monastic, once having experienced it, can never be the same. One is always wounded and weakened to things of a passing nature. But one is alive and energized for the things of the Realm of God. In short, one is a complete sacrifice for the salvation of others. One's own redemption does not finally matter. It is the Church and its mission which becomes more and more all consuming. For that is where the Body of Christ is. There is home and the place of God's glory.

CHAPTER SEVEN

Beyond the Gates:
Monasticism Past and Present

Having celebrated the heavenly liturgy in the vast assembly hall of the building, such as we glimpsed it in chapter one, and having completed the work of their charism, monastics now stand ready to exit the building where the Church had gathered and return to the world. They must pass through circles of scoffers, who are also making their way out of the hall with noise and no reverence. The monastics skirt their jabs and their harsh and pointed comments. They have no hooks on which anyone can hang anything. They slip noiselessly out of the hall in twos or threes and come into the atrium. There, they are not tempted by the amusements nor by any of the acquaintances they encounter. Attracting no attention to themselves, yet moving quickly and with purpose through the throng still enjoying its leisure on the glistening brown red floor, the monastics make their way to the exits of the building and meld into the crowds on the street.

Their exit from the building means that they are leaving, in a certain qualified sense, their monasticism. In fact, they are making of it an offering. How could they hold on to anything when the whole of their training has insisted that everything must be given up in the end, even good things? And if they are not sacrificing their way of life, at least, they are willing to let it be broken into by the Church. Apparently, they are willing to make the ultimate sacrifice for Christ. Who has asked this offering of them?

The Holy Spirit asks this sacrifice of the monastics. But in making his request, the Spirit has also moved monasticism into a new place by shifting the axis of salvation history in favor of the baptized toward the close of the second millennium thanks to the Vatican Council. Both the council and the cataclysmic events of this century urge us on to a new vision of things where the lessons of the gospel, preserved by the monastic church, have new relevance. We must look to the past, and see the familiar things, but in an angle of light that is new. Equipped with this knowledge, we must trace out our future path with renewed energy and confidence.

What we have attempted to do in the preceding chapters is to put a new face on some very old teaching. Whether this attempt fails or succeeds matters not. For many have already succeeded in bringing the monastic tradition forward through the centuries. Everything in our past points to the fact that monasticism will again be adapted to the present and the future. Though monasticism seems to be a bedrock of tradition, it has nevertheless changed a great deal. It has dialogued with many different cultures simultaneously and successively throughout the Christian and now post-Christian eras. It has found permanence, not in its customs or observances, for these are many and varied; but it has found its identity in the charism of the Holy Spirit. God has freshly gifted the Church with monasticism through all the Church's times and expressions. This, in fact, is our permanence.

The Place of the Contemplative

In the same way as God's gift to the Church is different, but enduring and the same, so, too, in the life of the individual monastic, the gift of a vocation is a great journey of many arrivals and departures. One's life differs vastly from the first years of formation to the time of harvest and beyond, yet it preserves the first call with its original ideals and grace. The monastic becomes a contemplative when he or she holds within the self the paradox between self-fulfillment and self-sacrifice. Obviously, the paradox is manifested right in the monastic community, where the monastic's own humble life contributes to the good of the others and the community. There, one bonds effectively with the community where honor, freely given and received, transforms one into a lover of the place, as St. Stephen Harding was called by his brothers at early Cîteaux. The monastic community itself, however, celebrates its own paradox when it appears to be separated from the society in a self-seeking way, only to hold an imperative place at the heart of the commonweal. The contemplative and the monastic community do not just float freely about at the edge of secular society. Sociologically, they hug the periphery; but, metaphysically, they are rooted in the very heart of humanity because of the place they occupy in the Church. The monk is inserted in the monastic community by the imitation of Christ. But the monastery is part of the Church, the body of Christ, because of the baptism into Christ of its members. The monastic community is a Church in its own right, and is thereby inserted into the Church universal, whose confines, in space or time, no one can fix. As such, the body of Christ is the transcendent horizon of our humanity. Much more than a concept of infinity for the human spirit, the Church is the real and living presence of the divine and human Christ—the same Christ who took on our flesh, suffered, died and rose from the dead on this earth. The contemplative in the Church is present to the whole world, not by desire, or social or prophetic stance, but by an insertion into the body of Christ, and by a particular position in that body.

The Church allows the monastic-contemplative to assume a stance of prophecy and forgiveness for the society at large. But that position is only the beginning of the contemplative's role. For the Church itself is a sign of salvation for the whole human family. The monastic community shares in that sign by means of its own special charism. Its sign is to point to the human heart where all the contradiction begins. Refusing to assign the blame anywhere else, and refusing to settle for any other solution than the most radical one, the contemplative becomes a sign of the conversion of the human heart. This sacrament plays on the stage of trial, where every person falls in a helpless faint at the challenge of doing right. We speak here of a weakness which stands at the back of the human conscience and which binds everyone together on a level fathoms deep and invisible, but known by the purity of one's actions and the look in one's eye. The contemplative goes to those depths where dreams speak the truth, and the stream of consciousness betrays a person in a Freudian slip. Christ spoke of this "place" of truth when He said to his disciples: "Nothing is covered up that will not be uncovered, and nothing secret that will not become known. Therefore whatever you have said in the dark will be heard in the light, and what you have whispered behind closed doors will be proclaimed from the housetops" (Luke 12:2-3).

The "place" of the contemplative is the depths of the human heart, where we turn from God in shame at our deeds, or embrace God in faith and trust. In the crucible of conscience, we all know and see one another; there we discover Christ. We look to Christ, the contemplative, for a countenance of truth and liberation, and for reassurance that humanity cannot reach its goal without putting on his own unique and unqualified obedience. Our "place" is in that heart of Christ, and our lives are signs pointing to his ultimate meaning.

Lovers of the Place

The place of the monastics, though they seem to have given it up, remains secure. For, having been purified, having died with Christ, their place is now with him. His place is everywhere, in every heart that looks to the Supreme Being for love and life. Having loved the place he first gave them, and having followed the Lamb wherever he goes, they now find that place to be infinitely wider than any geographic place. With the vow of stability still intact, though not in the eyes of the small-minded, the place which they love is now the world for which Christ died. Here is ascesis, prayer, contemplation and cloister. Here is home, examen and discretion. Yet here also is the noble human family housed in a place of wealth, and the monastics serve that palatial home like servants from the carriage house out back. Here the monastics bless and approve, affirm and take notice, even as their ministry is hidden.

If the term **place** becomes so rich as to be infinite, so also the term **number** takes on a noncountable character. So the number of monastic doctrines, though multiplied through the centuries, becomes almost infinite. And in their complexity, they become simple. As rich as the monastic tradition is, it can be seen in a nutshell of reduction. It reduces so easily, because its tenets are so simple; development of its doctrine would seem to be infinite. The number "three," or its multiples, or the number "seven," or even "one," "ten" or "twelve" all symbolize the fact that the monastic doctrine is not merely the addition of teachings which when added together make up an identifiable number. Each of the teachings can be used to arrive at that one doctrine which pursues the Trinity itself. Thus, the numerical symbolism in this work suggests that the real truth of monastic doctrine is somewhere in these words, but is hardly identifiable in any one place, simply because the teachings cannot be laid out in numerical sequence, nor can they be counted as such, nor can they be located definitely anywhere along the spiritual journey. In the same way, Evagrius described the Trinity: "The three of numbers is obtained by the addition of units but the Holy Trinity does not exist by addition of numbers because it is not a three of numbers."[1]

But in the living of the whole of the monastic doctrine, we find Christ, who deigned to come among us in the numerical sequence of time. Number symbolism, thus, attempts to point beyond human calculation to the divine hidden in them, just as Christ clothed himself in our humanity. Monastic doctrine is to know Christ and the power of his resurrection. It is to redefine the term **place** because, after his resurrection, the place of his glory is there where he is present with the power of his teaching and his person. My place becomes his place. Thus I know my own death and life, and the opposites which only he can reconcile even as I know others in their death and life. And I must be present to them as he is present—in his resurrection. To be both high and low, rich and poor, alive and dead, strong and weak, for the sake of others, for the sake of creation and its joy and beauty,

---

[1] Evagrius Ponticus, *Kephalaia Gnostica*, ed. Antoine Guillaumont, *Patrologia orientalis* XXVIII fasc. 1 n. 134, "Sixth Century," S2, n. 13, p. 221. The English version is from an unpublished translation.

is to be much more than my mind can conceive, much more than opposites, but not enough for what my heart desires.

Obviously, there are no short cuts to this kind of love of the place. What we have described is not a new monasticism which is temporary in character. That would be to misunderstand the inflexible and unyielding training that a monastic endures. Nor are we preaching a monasticism that is watered down and thinned into oblivion for the sake of the crowd. That would belittle the gifts of the Spirit given with such superabundance all through the centuries.

But we are defining monasticism's place in the Church in the light of *Lumen gentium* where a major shift in ecclesiology has taken place. Monasticism, as one of the earliest and perhaps the most fruitful charism in the long history of the Church, should be the first to stand up and be counted in this reconfigured assembly. Our response should be to return to the Church what we have been given. With all the gifts intact, and after years of formation, at least some should return to the Church in an act of self giving for the sake of the kingdom of God. If the Church can point herself onto a road of such different direction, so can monasticism follow without losing an iota of the monastic charism except what the heat of the gospel can burn away.

Not only are we suggesting that some monastics return to the wider Church from the cloister, but that, in the light of a new vision of the Church, the monastic tradition should share its riches more easily with the Church under the guidance of the bishops, as Paul VI repeatedly asked. In the vast assembly hall where the heavenly liturgy takes place, the monastics are in full and tantalizing view of everyone who is thirsting for God. Both the monastics and the rest of the Church are challenged by that renewed congregation. One must give and the other must take, so that both can come together. What was marginal must come home. And what was disdained as radical must be properly digested. A more obvious sharing of gifts and a more comprehensive benediction of the world must take place within and without the vast assembly hall which is the Church.

The New Evangelization

The Vatican Council, especially in its two ground breaking documents, *Lumen gentium* and *Gaudium et spes*, has indicated the need for a new ecclesiology. For religious, the documents of renewal have not been enough, coming so soon as they did after the council. Decades will have to pass before the full import of the council's challenge can be digested and internalized. The monastic charism itself has become ripe on the vine, with so many of its gifts intact and ready for harvesting. The need for sharing among the various segments of the Church has moved from luxury to necessity, given the enormity of the scope of the worldwide problems which face us today. All across the Church, a new theology suggests itself which sees more and more that the place of God's glory is where the risen Christ is present and acting. The glory of God emerges even when the cup of cold water is given from the depths of the heart for the sake of Christ. It appears when heartbreaking courtesy gets lavished on the oppressed and the insignificant because Jesus taught us to do so. Therefore, we seek a spirituality of new moral refinement which issues forth in a theology of the glory of God. All these elements, where they are present in our Church today, are presuppositions for a new evangelization of the world. Obviously, such a creative effort can only be accomplished by a renewed Church. And we are just in time. Never before has the world been so united and ready to listen, when former systems which promised a material salvation, have failed. Communism is but the latest failure, to say nothing about the various religious wars which bring into question religion itself. Never before, perhaps, has the world's people so needed and sought out a message of salvation. Never before have the challenges of religious fundamentalism, on the one side, and atheism, on the other, claimed such numbers of people. The Church will not be equipped to meet such difficulties unless it should reach deep down into its treasure house and bring up from there the most ancient wisdom she has, which is, surprisingly, fresh and fragrant with the gospel. But ancient springs can flow into new cisterns only with difficulty. Yet newly constructed waterways can handle the swift flowing waters of today's monasticism, which is both ancient and new, as is Christ himself.

The Holy Spirit, who gave the charism in the first place, is seen now to be giving it again in new or adapted forms. And if one is to be true to the Spirit, one must be ready to notice the marks of his presence. So, we observe that the monastics leave the building almost totally unheralded. They are not tempted by vainglory or vanity of any sort. Their decision has been long in coming. They are leaving the building only after long deliberation and after their piercing by the transfigured light at the climax of the liturgy. So drained are they of color, signifying their self-emptying, that their exit is visually minimal. They leave with no bitterness produced from anger or resentment. Nor does any desire to avoid unpleasantness motivate them. They know what they are likely to face on the street. The delights outside, both of sight and sound, to say nothing of taste and pleasure, hold no attractions. Their discipline is firm. If anything they dread the darts of temptation which they must endure again. Their decision is not a reasoned one. Only the Spirit's reasons are known. Human calculation would have counselled otherwise. But since the monastics have been burnt with the glory of the "place," they now seek that glory wherever it may be found. Bypassing structures, methods and customs which the current scene holds dear, they seek out the glory of God in the silence of untrumpeted love. They keep alive the larger dimension of life when everyone else sees only the details. They see the forest and the trees in the right perspective. They see the human person stretched in a tension of glory between heaven and earth. The glory of God is to be seen only occasionally where the media sees excitement. As grace extends to more and more people, and the glory of Christ shines forth, as if on Tabor, where the gospel is lived for its own sake, even behind closed doors, so there you will find the Church, and the monastics in attendance for a glimpse of it.

Further Reading in Monastic Spirituality

Ancient Authors

Apophthegmata Patrum

> *The Sayings of the Desert Fathers: The Alphabetical Collection.* Trans. Benedicta Ward, S.L.G. London: Mowbrays, 1975.
>
> *The Desert Fathers.* Trans. Helen Waddell. New York: Sheed and Ward, 1936.

Athanasius

> *The Life of Anthony and the Letter to Marcellinus.* Trans. Robert C. Gregg. Classics of Western Spirituality (CWS). New York: Paulist Press, 1980.

Basil

> *Ascetical Works.* Trans. M. Monica Wagner. FC 9. Washington, D.C.: The Catholic University of America (CUA) Press, 1950.

Benedict of Nursia

> *RB 1980: The Rule of St. Benedict.* Ed. Timothy Fry, O.S.B. Collegeville, Minn.: The Liturgical Press, 1981.

Cassian

> *The Institutes and Conferences.* Trans. Edgar C. S. Gibson. Nicene and Post-Nicene Fathers, vol. 11. Grand Rapids, Mich.: Eerdmans, 1964.
>
> *Conferences.* Trans. Colm Luibheid. Classics of Western Spirituality (CWS). New York: Paulist Press, 1985.

Evagrius Ponticus

> *Evagrius Ponticus: The Praktikos: Chapters on Prayer.* Trans. John Eudes Bamberger. Cistercian Studies 4. Spencer, Mass.: Cistercian Publications, 1972.
>
> *The "Ad Monachos" of Evagrius Ponticus: Its Structure and a Select Commentary.* Driscoll, Jeremy, O.S.B. Rome: *Studia Anselmiana* 104 (1991).
>
> *The Mind's Long Journey to the Holy Trinity: The* Ad Monachos *of Evagrius Ponticus.* Trans. and intro. Jeremy Driscoll, O.S.B. Collegeville: The Liturgical Press, 1993.

Gregory the Great

> *Dialogues.* Trans. Odo J. Zimmerman. Washington, D.C.: The Catholic University of America (CUA) Press, 1959.
>
> *The Life and Miracles of St. Benedict: Book Two of the Dialogues.* Trans. Odo J. Zimmerman and Benedict Avery. Collegeville, Minn.: The Liturgical Press, 1949.
>
> *The Life of Saint Benedict.* Trans. Hilary Costello and Eoin de Bhaldraithe. Commentary by Adalbert de Vogüé. Petersham, Mass.: St. Bede Publications, 1993.
>
> *Pastoral Care.* Trans. and annotated Henry Davis, S.J. Ancient Christian Writers (ACW) 11. Westminster, Md.: Newman Press, 1955.

John Climacus

> *The Ladder of Divine Ascent.* Trans. Colm Luibheid and Norman Russell. Classics of Western Spirituality (CWS). New York: Paulist Press, 1957.

Origen

> *The Song of Songs: Commentary and Homilies.* Trans. and annotated R. P. Lawson. Ancient Christian Writers (ACW) 26. Westminster, Md.: Newman Press, 1957.

Pachomius

> *Pachomian Koinonia. Vol. I: The Life of St. Pachomius and His Disciples.* Trans. Armand Veilleux, O.C.S.O. CS 45. Kalamazoo, Mich.: Cistercian Publications, 1980.
>
> *Pachomian Koinonia. Vol. II: Pachomian Chronicles and Rules.* Trans. Armand Veilleux, O.C.S.O. Cistercian Studies 46. Kalamazoo, Mich.: Cistercian Publications, 1981.
>
> *Pachomian Koinonia. Vol. III: Instructions, Letters, and Other Writings of St. Pachomius and His Disciples.* Trans. Armand Veilleux,

O.C.S.O. Cistercian Studies 47. Kalamazoo, Mich.: Cistercian Publications, 1982.

Cistercian Authors

Aelred of Rievaulx

> *Mirror of Charity.* Trans. Elizabeth Connor, O.C.S.O. Cistercian Fathers Series 17. Kalamazoo, Mich.: Cistercian Publications, 1990.
> *Spiritual Friendship.* Trans. Mary Eugenia Laker, S.S.N.D. Cistercian Fathers Series 5. Washington, D.C.: Cistercian Publications, 1974.

Bernard of Clairvaux

> *On Loving God.* Trans. Robert Walton, O.S.B. Cistercian Fathers Series 13B. Kalamazoo, Mich.: Cistercian Publications, 1994.
> *On Precept and Dispensation. (Treatises I)* Trans. Conrad Greenia, O.C.S.O. Cistercian Fathers Series 1. Spencer, Mass.: Cistercian Publications, 1970.
> *On the Song of Songs I.* (Sermons 1–20) Trans. Kilian Walsh, O.C.S.O. Cistercian Fathers Series 4. Spencer, Mass.: Cistercian Publications, 1971.
> *On the Song of Songs II.* (Sermons 21–46) Trans. Kilian Walsh, O.C.S.O. Cistercian Fathers Series 7. Kalamazoo, Mich.: Cistercian Publications, 1976.
> *On the Song of Songs III.* (Sermons 47–66) Trans. Kilian Walsh, O.C.S.O., and Irene M. Edmonds. Cistercian Fathers Series 31. Kalamazoo, Mich.: Cistercian Publications, 1979.
> *On the Song of Songs IV.* (Sermons 67–86) Trans. Irene M. Edmonds. Cistercian Fathers Series 40. Kalamazoo, Mich.: Cistercian Publications, 1980.
> *The Steps of Humility and Pride.* Trans. M. Ambrose Conway, O.C.S.O. Cistercian Fathers Series 13A. Kalamazoo, Mich.: Cistercian Publications, 1989.

Guerric of Igny

> *The Liturgical Sermons: Vol. 1.* Trans. Hilary Costello, O.C.S.O., and John Morson, O.C.S.O. Cistercian Fathers Series 8. Spencer, Mass.: Cistercian Publications, 1971.
> *The Liturgical Sermons: Vol. 2.* Trans. Hilary Costello, O.C.S.O., and John Morson, O.C.S.O. Cistercian Fathers Series 32. Spencer, Mass.: Cistercian Publications, 1971.

William of St. Thierry

> *The Golden Epistle: A Letter to the Brethren at Mont Dieu.* Trans. Theodore Berkeley, O.C.S.O. Cistercian Fathers Series 12. Spencer, Mass.: Cistercian Publications, 1971.

Contemporary Authors

Burrows, Ruth. *Guidelines for Mystical Prayer.* London: Sheed and Ward, 1976.

Butler, Cuthbert, O.S.B. *Western Mysticism.* New York: Dutton, 1923.

Casey, Michael, O.C.S.O *Athirst for God: Spiritual Desire in Bernard of Clairvaux's Sermon on the Song of Songs.* Cistercian Studies 77. Kalamazoo, Mich.: Cistercian Publications, 1988.

_____. *Sacred Reading: The Ancient Art of Lection Divina.* Liguori, Mo.: Triumph Books, 1996.

Chitty, Derwas, J. *The Desert a City: Introduction to Egyptian and Palestinian Monasticism.* Oxford: Blackwell, 1966.

De Vogüé, Aldalbert, O.S.B. *The Rule of Saint Benedict: A Doctrinal and Spiritual Commentary.* Cistercian Studies 54. Kalamazoo, Mich.: Cistercian Publications, 1983.

Gilson, Etienne. *The Mystical Theology of St. Bernard.* Cistercian Studies 120. Kalamazoo, Mich.: Cistercian Publications, 1990.

Hausherr, Irénée, S.J. *Penthos: The Doctrine of Compunction in the Christian East.* Trans. Anselm Hufstader, O.S.B. Cistercian Studies Series 53. Kalamazoo, Mich.: Cistercian Publications, 1982.

Kelty, Matthew, O.C.S.O. *Aspects of the Monastic Calling.* Abbey of Gethsemani, 1975.

Leclercq, Jean, O.S.B. *The Love of Learning and the Desire for God: A Study of Monastic Culture.* Trans. Catharine Misrahi. New York: Fordham University Press, 1961.

Louf, André, O.C.S.O. *Teach Us to Pray: Learning a Little about God.* Trans. Hubert Hoskins. Chicago: Franciscan Herald Press, 1975.

_____. *The Cistercian Way.* Trans. Nivard Kinsella, O.C.S.O. Cistercian Studies 76. Kalamazoo, Mich.: Cistercian Publications, 1989.

Marmion, Columba, O.S.B. *Christ, the Ideal of the Monk.* St. Louis: Herder, 1929.

_____. *Christ, the Ideal of the Priest.* St. Louis: Herder, 1952.

_____. *Christ, the Life of the Soul.* St. Louis: Herder, 1925.

_____. *The English Letters.* Baltimore, Md.: Helicon, 1962.

McGinn, Bernard. *The Growth of Mysticism: Gregory the Great through the 12th Century*. New York: Crossroad, 1994.

Merton, Thomas. *The Monastic Journey*. Ed. Patrick Hart. Cistercian Studies 133. Kalamazoo, Mich.: Cistercian Publications, 1992. [Much of Merton's vast output is still in print and readily available. *All of it is recommended*.]

Index